Threading the Evaluation Needle

Also by Todd A. DeMitchell
Teachers and Their Unions: Labor Relations in Uncertain Times
Educators at the Bargaining Table: Successfully Negotiating a Contract that Works for All
Labor Relations in Education: Policies, Politics, and Practices
Negligence: What Principals Need to Know About Avoiding Liability

Also by Todd A. DeMitchell & Richard Fossey
The Challenges of Mandating School Uniforms in the Public Schools: Free Speech, Research, and Policy.
Student Dress Codes and the First Amendment: Legal Challenges and Policy Issues
The Limits of Law-Based School Reform: Vain Hopes and False Promises.

Also by Mark A. Paige
Building a Better Teacher: Underlying Value-Added Models in the Law of Teacher Evaluation

Threading the Evaluation Needle

The Documentation of Teacher Unprofessional Conduct

Todd A. DeMitchell and Mark A. Paige

ROWMAN & LITTLEFIELD
Lanham • Boulder • New York • London

Published by Lexington Books
An imprint of The Rowman & Littlefield Publishing Group, Inc.
4501 Forbes Boulevard, Suite 200, Lanham, Maryland 20706
www.rowman.com

6 Tinworth Street, London SE11 5AL, United Kingdom

Copyright © 2020 by Todd A. DeMitchell and Mark A. Paige

All rights reserved. No part of this book may be reproduced in any form or by any electronic or mechanical means, including information storage and retrieval systems, without written permission from the publisher, except by a reviewer who may quote passages in a review.

British Library Cataloguing in Publication Information Available

Library of Congress Cataloging-in-Publication Data Available

ISBN 978-1-4758-5404-6 (cloth)
ISBN 978-1-4758-5405-3 (pbk.)
ISBN 978-1-4758-5406-0 (electronic)

Contents

Acknowledgments		vii
Preface: Who Shall Teach Our Children?		ix
A Tale of Two Teachers: Skill and Will in Documentation		ix
The Importance of Who Teaches		xi
1	Evaluation and the Documentation Challenge	1
2	The Evaluation of Teachers	5
3	The Principal as Evaluator	9
	Peer Assistance and Review Programs and Documentation	14
	Concluding Comments	15
4	Legal Frameworks: Infusing the Evaluation with Fairness	21
	What is Due Process?	21
	What Process is Due?	23
	Progressive Discipline and Just Cause	25
	Dismissal and Nonrenewal	27
	An Induced Exit	27
	Concluding Thoughts on the Approach of the Principal	29
5	The Five Fatal "Eyes" of Unprofessional Conduct	33
	Professional Codes of Ethics	33
	The Teacher as a Professional	35
	The Five Fatal "Eyes" of the Unprofessional Conduct	
	of Educators	37
	Inappropriate Conduct with Students	37
	Illegality	38
	Immorality	38

	Incompetence	39
	Insubordination	40
6	**Files, Memos, and Documentation**	**45**
	Documentation	46
	A. Notes to File: From Informal Communication to	
	Formal Documentation	46
	1. The Background	47
	2. Principal's Notes to File	47
	3. Principal's General Communication File	48
	4. Documentation Placed in the Personnel File	48
	Single Incident Memorandum	50
	Lakeside Middle School	50
	Remediation Memorandum	53
	Sample Ninety-Day Incompetency Progress Meeting	
	Memorandum	55
7	**Conclusion and the Ten Commandments of Documentation**	**61**
	The Ten Commandments of Documentation	62
Appendix: Tool Box Documents		**69**
	Document A: InTASC Model Core Teaching Standards and	
	Learning Progressions for Teachers	69
	Document B: Personnel Evaluation Standards	71
	Document C: Examples of Causes and Evidence for	
	Dismissal/Discipline	71
	Document D: The Bologna Sandwich Technique	74
	Document E: Negligent Hiring: Did We Hire the Wrong Person?	75
	Document F: Table of Cases	78
About the Authors		**85**

Acknowledgments

As always, I acknowledge the impact and untold number of contributions that Terri, my wife, makes to my personal life as well as my professional life. Her work as a school law attorney, informed by her experience as an elementary school teacher, shapes my work. I also wish to thank the school administrators and teachers with whom, over the past three decades, I have shared classes, read their papers, enjoyed their lively discussions, and benefitted from their insightful comments about the importance and the challenges of documenting professional behavior. They always kept me grounded on how the ethics of the profession should inform our decisions that impact the real lives of educators.

Todd A. DeMitchell

To Laura, my wife: thank you. Balancing a busy home with three young children and two careers (plus a dog, of course) is not easy. But we are succeeding, together! To my three children, Madeleine, Maeve, and Nell: Watching you all grow and mature is inspiration and motivation to all my work, as a father and a professor.

Mark A. Paige

Preface
Who Shall Teach Our Children?

Since the beginning of formal public education in America, teachers have been evaluated in some way or another by school authorities.[1]

A TALE OF TWO TEACHERS: SKILL AND WILL IN DOCUMENTATION

One teacher was untenured and in her final year before the tenure decision had to be made. The other teacher was a twenty-five-year veteran. One was an elementary school teacher and the other was secondary school teacher; both went through an evaluation process based on effective documentation. The evaluation needle was threaded with two different threads and two different outcomes; both had positive ends for students. Their true tales provide bookends to the importance of documentation and educational leaders who demonstrated both the skill and the will to only retain effective teachers in their school's classrooms.

The elementary school teacher was having problems with the organization of the class tasks and rhythms, classroom control, and had a disorganized instructional program. The principal identified the problems and support was sought from the district office. Careful records were kept, observations made, meetings held, resources provided (professional readings and expert professional colleagues), and a consistent clear message was communicated that we want you to succeed and will help you to succeed. But that it is your responsibility to meet the professional standards.

The other teacher was a veteran with one year of experience repeated twenty-five times. Her or his problems included poor classroom organization, poorly constructed and delivered instruction, and poor communications with parents. There was little enthusiasm in the class for teaching and learning. There was a sense that everyone was marking time until all could move on to something important. Class was a time to endure and wait out until the minute hand moved. "This too shall pass," was a frequently mumbled phrase by the teacher and the students. Tumult, chaos, and lethargy often characterized the classroom climate. A lack of discipline, civility, and respect pervaded almost daily class sessions.

The high school's new principal took pride in and worked hard to instill a sense that professional practice and demeanor was expected and valued. Her commitment to high expectations was unwavering. She identified and stepped up her observations from the beginning of the teacher's request to transfer to her school, resulting in documentation of the teacher's practice that was clear, concise, and backed up by evidence.

At the conclusion of the first year, she requested support for instituting a remediation plan for the upcoming year. The district office worked closely with the principal to identify the deficiencies and to develop a plan of action to appropriately address them. By the start of the second semester the remediation plan was ratcheted it up to meet the state law requirements for an official notice of incompetency with a specific timeline for resolution.

The union was kept informed. Union officials often act as private allies seeking to only have competent colleagues in the schools, and public adversaries fulfilling their duty to represent teachers in fair proceedings.[2] Meetings were held with the teacher, the union, the principal and the director of personnel & labor relations. Documentation of observations, parent communications, and progress towards proficiency via the remediation plan, were shared and discussed. The last meeting saw a breakthrough when the district office administrator stated that the State's Education Code required a notification be sent to the Department of Education if a teacher was dismissed for incompetency.

The first tale ended with the teacher meeting the expected standards and attaining tenure. The teacher continued to hone her or his professional practice. The principal, a year later, used an aspect of the teacher's practice as an example of a successful instructional approach during a professional development activity. The teacher was becoming an accomplished professional.

The second tale ended differently. The teacher chose to resign, essentially an induced exit (see Chapter 4) in the face of the certainty of a recommendation for dismissal.

In both instances, the principals employed an effective documentation system demonstrating the skill and the will to only place and etain effective educators in their school's classrooms. School leaders and district leaders shared a common value and worked together to actualize that value in the classrooms of their schools. In the first case, the potential of a teacher was sought, with clear support, and the teacher's sincere efforts to develop the professional skills so as to benefit her or his students. *In the second case, the ineffectiveness of the teacher was identified and when the offered support did not result in effective practice, the teacher was induced to depart In both situations, students were well served.*

THE IMPORTANCE OF WHO TEACHES

The common school, however humble its surroundings or deficient its curriculum, is the most valuable public institution in the state.
Williams v. Stanton Common School District, 173 Ky 798, 798 (1893).

The importance of an educated citizenry to a society is one of the few uncontested beliefs. The Supreme Court recognized this almost forty years ago writing, "[E]ducation provides the basic tools by which individuals might lead economically productive lives to the benefit of us all. In sum, education has a fundamental role in maintaining the fabric of our society."[3] Therefore, the education of the citizenry, primarily through our system of public schools, is critical to the health of our democracy.

It follows that being educated is important in the lives of individuals. Education opens gates and its absence closes gates. Teachers, to a large extent, hold the keys to those gates. Whom we place and keep in the classroom has an effect on the future of the students in that classroom. Consequently, the challenges are to only place and keep quality teachers in front of those students. This requires principals, who are charged with the efficient operation of the school, to discharge their duties in a professional and legal manner. Their duty of supervision and evaluation is critical to the success of students.

The current climate of education policy deliberations, especially regarding tenure protections,[4] has placed teacher effectiveness front and center in the policy debate about how to improve student achievement and how to hold schools and teachers accountable for that achievement. Teacher evaluation as part of accountability systems has become a strategy for improving teacher effectiveness and, thus, improving student performance. However, underlining the importance of evaluations, documentation has emerged as an integral part of those evaluations. However, a briefing paper from the Economic Policy Institute characterizes schools as doing a "poor job of systematically developing and evaluating teachers."[5]

Teacher evaluation impacts student achievement. It also impacts teachers. The greater the stakes of the evaluation—salary, tenure, reduction-in-force, and dismissal decisions—the greater the impact on the professional lives of the teacher. Evaluation influences "whether teachers are drawn to and remain in the profession."[6] A fair system of teacher evaluation with a relevant and effective system of documentation to support the evaluation is necessary in this high stakes environment.

A dismissal can have devastating effects on an individual[7] and is critically important to the school. Principals are on the front lines of gathering information, documenting teacher practices, conferencing with the teacher, and formulating a high stakes recommendation. Law, ethics, and professional practice comingle in the stream that leads to a decision to dismiss or retain. "The firing of a teacher takes place at a high personal cost—not only to the teacher, but also to the principal."[8] Principals need as much skill as they can gain and graft those skills to their will to act, and to their professional sense of what action supports their students.

This book seeks to add to and inform the policy and practices of principals and other supervisors who place and retain effective educators in all of our classrooms. If teachers matter, then how school officials recruit, supervise, and evaluate them so as to place an effective teaching force in our classrooms matters.

We bring over two decades of experience in the public schools in teaching and administrative positions and over four decades in higher education where we teach school law, human resources, and labor relations. Our approach to writing this book is informed by our experiences as teachers, a school law attorney, a principal, director of personnel and labor relations, and superintendent. We hope that your time spent with our book increases your understanding of documentation and adds to your skill in providing documentation that fairly, ethically, and effectively informs your practice.

NOTES

1. Lawrence F. Rossow & Laural Logan-Fein, *The Law of Teacher Evaluation* (3rd Ed.) (Dayton, OH: Education Law Association 2013), 1.

2. See Todd A. DeMitchell, "A Reinvented Union: A Concern for Teaching and Not Just Teachers" *Journal of Personnel Evaluation in Education* 11 (1998): 255–68, 262–65.

3. *Plyler v. Doe*, 457 U.S. 202, 221 (1982). Expanding on the importance of education, the Court writes, "The American people have always regarded education and the acquisition of knowledge as matters of extreme importance. We have recognized the public schools as a most vital civic institution for the preservation of a democratic system of government and as the primary vehicle for transmitting the values on which our society rests" *Id.*

4. The following two quotes help to frame the arguments on both sides of the tenure debate.

    Rick Perry, Former Texas Governor stated, "Good teachers know they don't need tenure. There is no reason to have it except to protect those that don't perform as they should." (Trip Gabriel & Sam Dillon, "G.O.P. Governors Take Aim at Teacher Tenure." *The New York Times* (January 31, 2011), Site visited August 9, 2016, http://www.nytimes.com/2011/02/01/us/01tenure.html?_r=1.

Professor McNeal notes, as the U.S. Supreme Court asserted in *Cleveland Board. of Education v. Loudermill*, 470 U.S. 532 (1985), "Tenure, as originally designed, only protects teachers from frivolous dismissals, not for legitimate reasons such as incompetence, inadequate performance, immoral conduct, insubordination, willful neglect of duties, or any other sufficient cause." (Laura McNeal, "Total Recall: The Rise and Fall of Teacher Tenure" *Hofstra Labor & Employment Law Journal* 30 (2013): 489–510, 509.

Benjamin M. Superfine and Jessica J. Gottlieb, "Teacher Evaluation and Collective Bargaining: The New Frontier of Civil Rights." *Michigan State Law Review* 2014 (2014): 737–88, 751.

5. Eva L. Baker, Paul E. Barton, Linda Darling-Hammond, Edward Haertel, Helen F. Ladd, Robert L. Linn, Diane Ravitch, Richard Rothstein, Richard Shavelson, and Lorrie A. Sheppard. (August 29, 2010). *Problems With the Use of Student Test Scores to Evaluate Teachers.* (Washington, DC: Economic Policy Institute), 1.

6. Jodi Wood Jewell, "From Inspection, Supervision, and Observation to Value-Added Evaluation: A Brief History of U.S. Teacher Performance Evaluation." *Drake Law Journal* 65 (2017): 363–419, 415.

7. "Employment counselors have seen the devastating financial and psychological effects that getting fired has on a person's life. In fact, the trauma usually centers on the individual's self-concept. Feelings of inadequacy, failure, self-contempt, and anger are common to people who have their employment terminated." Ronald W. Rebore, *The Essentials of Human Resources Administration in Education* (Boston: Pearson 2012), 131.

8. David W. Messer, *The Impact of Dismissal of Non-Tenured Teachers on Principals in Tennessee* (East Tennessee State University: Unpublished doctoral dissertation 2001), 25. Site visited June 16, 2019, available at https://dc.etsu.edu/cgi/viewcontent.cgi?article=1135&context=etd.

Chapter 1

Evaluation and the Documentation Challenge

> Most teachers in our nation's schools are competent, conscientious, hardworking individuals. All too often their efforts are overshadowed by the poor performance of a relatively small number of incompetent classroom teachers. These incompetents must be identified and assisted, and if they fail to improve, dismissed.[1]

"Who shall teach our children?" is one of the great recurring, enduring, and important education questions since at least from the time that Socrates was sentenced to death for "corrupting the youth" of Athens with his teaching. The rise of the Common School Movement, the template for our current system of public schooling starting in the decades after the War of 1812, identified the professionalization of the teaching force as a key aspect of the public schools. Horace Mann, a leader in the newly emerging model of public education, instituted "normal schools" designed to provide teacher training.

Teachers occupy the pivotal position in the school; they stand at the crossroads of education—the "centrality of quality teachers to educational outcomes is intuitive."[2] It is largely through their efforts that the goals of education are achieved or thwarted. At the core of their work, teachers provide instruction, structure-learning activities, and assess the work of students.[3] All other activities at the school are primarily designed to support, augment, and extend the primacy of the essential teacher-student instructional interaction.

"It is well established that teacher quality makes a difference in student learning."[4] For educators this is an article of faith. The teacher working with students is the core of a school. Most of what is of sustained value that happens in a school occurs in an interaction between a student and an educator. Joseph M. Carroll writes, "Nothing, absolutely nothing has happened in education until it has happened to a student."[5] Therefore, what teachers do in their classrooms is central to the effectiveness of the state's system of public education as well as in private education.

Teachers make a difference in the education of a student. That difference cuts both ways; an effective teacher makes a difference in a student's learning and an ineffective teacher also makes a difference, just the wrong difference. As Harvard education professor Susan Moore Johnson wrote almost three decades ago, but with the same salience today, "Who teaches matters."[6] While the great majority of teachers are dedicated, accomplished professionals who serve the best interests of their students, some teachers are ineffective.

Therefore, whom to place in front of students in a classroom, how to assist that teacher to reach higher levels of performance, when and how to identify deficiencies, and when to dismiss them are critical decisions. The U.S. Supreme Court in 1952 declared "that school authorities have the right and the duty to screen the officials, teachers, and employees as to their fitness to maintain the integrity of schools as a part of ordered society cannot be doubted."[7]

As Professors L. Dean Webb and M. Scott Norton write, "Performance evaluation is important to the internal operation and effectiveness of the school system and to the public's perception of the school system."[8] If teachers matter, then the policies and practices that structure their recruitment, selection, and retention matter, which includes a sound performance evaluation system (see Tool Box Document B for personnel evaluation standards).

"Policymakers are increasingly turning to evaluation and accountability for individual teachers as a way to improve school performance and student outcomes."[9] Teacher evaluations have become a major policy lever for reform. In the last decade there has been a wave of state level legislation aimed at teacher evaluation as a means to increase accountability. From around 2009 almost three-dozen states have tied teacher evaluation to student achievement.[10] An important part of an evaluation is the documentation that supports the conclusion(s) of the evaluation.

Based on the research reviewed, it is recommended that policymakers employ an assessment system that targets both continual improvement of the teaching staff and timely dismissal of teachers who cannot or will not improve.

Patricia H. Hinchey, *Getting Teacher Assessment Right: What Policymakers Can Learn From Research.* (Boulder, CO: National Education Policy Center, Boulder, CO. December. 2010), Executive Summary. Site visited on August 9, 2015 available at https://nepc.colorado.edu/sites/def ault/files/PB-TEval-Hinchey_0.pdf.

This book reviews a critical and often difficult component of only placing competent professional educators in classrooms—documentation. The process of evaluation, documentation, remediation, and dismissal are important in improving education. As Deal and Peterson note, "the termination of people who are not serving a student-centered mission is one way a school demonstrates what it values."[11] And if a termination is warranted, it must be effectively and fairly documented.

The introduction above identifies the central role of teachers in the achievement of their students; chapter 2 further explores that centrality. Teachers stand at the crossroads of a student's education helping to move them onto the freeways of life or shunting them to the byways and cul-de-sacs of life. Chapter 3 discusses the challenges that principals encounter in evaluating, identifying deficiencies, remediating those deficiencies, or dismissing teachers who do not meet standards of the profession. Chapter 4 reviews the legal frameworks for evaluation and dismissal. Specifically, due process and the structuring role it plays in the remediation and dismissal process as well as progressive discipline and just cause are explored. Chapter 5 explores the five fatal "Eyes" of unprofessional conduct. It posits that the majority of the causes for dismissal can be organized under five categories. Chapter 6 reviews the process of documenting behaviors. Suggestions for action and examples of documentation are provided. Chapter 7 concludes with a discussion of the Ten Commandments of documentation and some summary comments. A Tool Box of Documents is provided with more background information that seeks to inform the principal's practice and provide more depth for the researcher.

NOTES

1. Edwin M. Bridges, with the assistance of Barry Groves, *Managing the Incompetent Teacher* (2d ed.) (Eugene OR: Clearinghouse on Educational Management College of Education University of Oregon 1990) 8. Visited June 7, 2019 available at https://pdfs.semanticscholar.org/8ec8/014eb406c1b58f33d2c02e9d37287a356830.pdf

2. Derek W. Black, "The Constitutional Challenge to Teacher Tenure." *California Law Review* 104 (2016): 75–148, 83.

3. See Charlotte Danielson's framework for teaching. The four domains are (1) planning and preparation, (2) classroom environment, (3) instruction, and (4) professional responsibilities. Author, "The Framework," The Danielson Group (2017), https://www.danielsongroup.org/framework/; James H. Strong, Thomas J. Ward, & Leslie W. Grant, "What Makes Good Teachers Good? A Cross-Case Analysis of the Connection Between Teacher Effectiveness and Student Achievement." *Journal of Teacher Education* 62 (2011): 339–355, 351 (synthesizing their review of the

literature into four dimensions: instructional delivery, student assessment, learning environment, and personal qualities). Furthermore, they write, "The common denominator in school improvement and student success is the teacher."

4. Patricia H. Hinchey, *Getting Teacher Assessment Right: What Policymakers Can Learn From Research* (Boulder, CO: National Education Policy Center December, 2010), 1. Site visited on August 9, 2015, available at https://nepc.colorado.edu/sites/default/files/PB-TEval-Hinchey_0.pdf. See also, Jennifer K. Rice, *Teacher Quality: Understanding the Effectiveness of Teacher Attributes* (Washington, DC: Economic Policy Institute August 2003) (writing, "Teacher quality matters. In fact, it is the most important school-related factor influencing student achievement."), 1. Site visited on August 9, 2015, available at https://www.epi.org/publication/books_teacher_quality_execsum_intro/; Demetra Kalogrides, Suzanne Loeb, & Tara Beteille (March 2011). *Power Play? Teacher Characteristics and Class Assignments* (Washington, DC: National Center for Analysis of Longitudinal Data in Education Research, Calder the Urban Institute March 2011). Site visited on April 15, 2019, available at http://www.caldercenter.org/upload/CALDERWorkPaper_59.pdf (writing, "The effect of teachers on student achievement is particularly well established."), 1.

5. Joseph M. Carroll, *The Copernican Plan Evaluated: The Evolution of a Revolution* (Andover, MA: Regional Library for Educational Improvement of the Northeast and Islands 1994), 87.

6. Susan Moore Johnson, *Teachers at Work: Achieving Success in Our Schools* (New York, NY: Basic Books 1990), xii.

7. *Adler v. Board of Education*, 342 U.S. 485, 493 (1952).

8. L. Dean Webb and M. Scott Norton, *Human Resources Administration: Personnel Issues and Needs in Education* (5th Ed.) (Upper Saddle River, NJ: Pearson 2009), 191.

9. Douglas N. Harris, William K. Ingle, and Stacey A. Rutledge, "How Teacher Evaluation Methods Matter for Accountability: A Comparative Analysis of Teacher Effectiveness Ratings by Principals and Teacher Value-Added Measures." *American Educational Research Journal* 51 (February 2014): 73–112, 74.

10. Benjamin M. Superfine and Jessica J. Gottlieb, "Teacher Evaluation and Collective Bargaining: The New Frontier of Civil Rights." *Michigan State Law Review* 2014 (2014): 737–788, 751.

11. Terrence E. Deal and Kent D. Peterson, *The Leadership Paradox: Balancing Logic and Artistry in Schools* (Washington, DC: Wiley 1994), 79.

Chapter 2

The Evaluation of Teachers

> "[Just cause] must include the concept that a school district is not married to mediocrity but may dismiss personnel who are neither performing high-quality work nor improving in performance. On the other hand, '"just cause' cannot include reasons which are arbitrary, unfair, or generated out of some petty vendetta."[1]

The *Briggs* case, above, from forty years ago underscores the continued importance of conducting quality evaluations. The principal, Briggs, was dismissed in part for "inconsistent and superficial written evaluations of his teaching staff."[2] This challenge of conducting effective and fair evaluations persists. The ability of the principal to effectively employ documentation techniques that identify concerns about performance is critical in retaining effective teachers.

First, our beginning point is the acknowledgment of the critical role that teachers play in student achievement. Succinctly stated, the quality of the teacher matters.[3] All activities at the school are primarily designed to support, augment, and extend the primacy of the essential teacher-student instructional interaction. Consequently, "quality teaching plays a major, if not the most important, role in shaping students' academic performance."[4] Therefore, what teachers do in their classrooms is central to the effectiveness of the state's system of public education as well as in private education.

As we have stated above, current research consistently finds that the quality of the teacher is one of the most important determinants of a student's academic success. For example, Hanuschek states, "First, teachers are very important; no other measured aspect of schools is nearly as important in determining student achievement."[5]

Classroom educators' decisions are directed at assisting and guiding their students to meet and exceed the learning outcomes—educational, social, and personal—established by the school board. Educational researchers such as Strong, Ward, and Grant in their study of effective and ineffective classroom practices found that the dimensions of teacher effectiveness include instructional delivery, student assessment, establishing a suitable learning environment, and the possession of personal characters such as fairness, respect, and enthusiasm.[6] As stated above the teacher stands at the crossroads of a student's education.

Teachers occupy an important place in our society with their unique relationship with the community's children whether or not that concept is called *in loco parentis* or custodial and tutelary.[7] Parents trust their children to teachers through compulsory education laws through extended periods of time. No other professional activity outside of teaching has such extended control and influence over minors. And they exercise this control and influence with the full weight of a government bureaucracy to back them up. Parents and the community have a legitimate concern about the qualifications and actions of their teachers.

Therefore, excellence in schools is most directly related to the performance of educators acting in concert and individually. The evaluation of teachers is a critical component in the consistent delivery of a quality education to students—"it is pivotal to improving teacher quality."[8] Concomitantly, teachers have the right and the need to receive accurate and fair feedback. The purposes of the supervision/evaluation process include but are not limited to:

- Develop, improve, and maintain teaching skills and behaviors that result in students meeting stated outcomes/goals, and
- Provide a means for the identification and the resolution of problems in work performance, up to and including non-retention or dismissal.

The standards for teacher evaluations should define the essential elements of competence.[9] They hold individuals accountable for their practice by assisting them to improve; failure to improve may lead to dismissal. In other words, the teacher did not meet the accepted standards of practice for the teaching profession. The South Dakota Supreme Court wrote, "The purpose of any evaluation is to monitor changes in performance and make improvements where necessary."[10] Building effective, professional teacher evaluation systems is a critical policy concern.

Because of the high stakes nature of evaluations and its attending documentation techniques and practices, it is critical that the process be carried out in an ethical manner.[11] Researchers Carla M. Evans, Jade Caines (Lee), and Winston C. Thompson offer an insightful discussion about an ethical framework for teacher evaluations.[12] They assert that applied ethics "can help explain how individuals should be treated and on what basis decisions should be evaluated."[13] The researchers identify five key characteristics related to teacher evaluation policies. Evaluation policies, they assert, should apply these five ethical principles:

- Non-maleficence: not cause harm to teachers.[14]
- Beneficence: do good and benefit teachers and key stakeholders, balancing beneficial consequences against potentially harmful ones.
- Autonomy: recognize that teachers deserve respect and are possessed of rights.
- Justice: be fair.
- Fidelity: be honest and trustworthy.[15]

Ethical teacher evaluation policies coupled with the ethical application of the policy through the use of these principles should be an important part of the evaluation system and its documentation component.[16] As noted above, teachers are the core of the relationship with students and because of this role they must be treated in an ethical manner. Placing and retaining effective teachers in classrooms and removing ineffective teachers must be grounded in an ethical approach.

> We must focus less on how to rank and fire teachers and more on how to make day-to-day teaching an attractive, challenging job that intelligent, creative, and ambitious people will gravitate toward.
> Dana Goldstein, *The Teacher Wars: A History of America's Most Embattled Profession* (New York: Doubleday 2014), 11.

NOTES

1. *Briggs v. Board. of Directors. of Hinton Community School* District, 288 N.W.2d 740, 743 (Iowa 1979). For another case on the dismissal of a principal, see *Hayes v. Phoenix-Talent School District*, 893 F.2d 235 (9th Cir. 1990) in which a principal was dismissed for a "lack of tact" and an inability to get along with others.).

2. Ibid., 744.

3. Jesse Rothstein (May 2008). *Teacher Quality in Educational Production: Tracking, Decay, and Student Achievement* (Cambridge, MA: National Bureau of Economic Research May 2008). Site visited on May 18, 2019, available at https://www.nber.org/papers/w14442.pdf.

4. Jian Wang, Emily Lin, Elizabeth Spalding, Cari L. Klecka, and Sandra J. Odell, "Quality Teaching and Teacher Education: A Kaleidoscope of Notions." *Journal of Teacher Education* 62 (2011): 331–338, 338.

5. Eric A. Hanushek, *The Economic Value of Higher Teacher Quality* (Cambridge, MA: National Bureau of Economic Research December 2010), 3. Site visited on April 10, 2013, available at https://www.nber.org/papers/w16606.pdf.

6. James H. Strong, Thomas J. Ward, and Leslie W. Grant, "What Makes Good Teachers Good? A Cross-Case Analysis of the Connection Between Teacher Effectiveness and Student Achievement." *Journal of Teacher Education* 62 (2011): 339–355, 340–342.

7. *Vernonia School District 47J v. Acton*, 515 U.S. 646, 655 (1995).

8. Mark Paige and Perry A. Zirkel, "Teacher Evaluation at the Intersection of Age and Disability Discrimination: A Case Law Analysis" *Education Law & Policy Review* 1 (2014): 72–98, 74.

9. See, for example, Anthony T. Malinoski, Herbert G. Heneman III, and Steven M. Kimball, *Review of Teaching Performance Assessments for Use in Human Capital Management* (Madison, WI: Strategic Management in Human Capital, Consortium for Policy Research in Education August 2009), 6. Eight important teaching competencies that support the improvement of student learning are given below:

(1) Attention to Student Standards
(2) Use of Formative Assessment to Guide Instruction
(3) Differentiation of Instruction
(4) Engaging Students
(5) Use of Instructional Strategies that Develop Higher Order Thinking Skills
(6) Content Knowledge and Pedagogical Content Knowledge
(7) Development of Personalized Relationships with Students
(8) High Expectations for Students.

10. *Iverson v. Wall Bd. of Educ.*, 522 N.W. 2d 188, 193 (S.D. 1994).

11. Professor Audrey Amrein-Beardsley cautioned about using evaluation systems that adopt a theory of change based on Measure and Punish. Audrey Amrein-Beardsley, *Rethinking Value-Added Models in Education: Critical Perspectives on Tests and Assessment-Based Accountability* (Oxford, Great Britain: Taylor and Francis 2014).

12. Carla M. Evans, Jade Caines, and Winston C. Thompson, "First Do No Harm?: A Framework for Ethical Decision-Making in Teacher Evaluation," in Kimberly Kapper Hewitt and Audrey Amrein-Beardsley (eds.) *Student Growth Measures in Policy and Practice: Intended and Unintended Consequences of High Stakes Teacher Evaluations* (Switzerland: Springer 2016), 169–88.

13. Evans, et al., "First Do No Harm?," 176.

14. "Just because a teacher is upset about receiving a negative evaluation does not mean she/he was treated unethically. But, if it is the case that some teachers were misclassified or erroneously evaluated, then those teachers *have* been unduly harmed and actions may need to be revisited." (emphasis in original) Ibid., 177.

15. Ibid.

16. The New Hampshire Code of Conduct (ED 510) can be accessed at https://www.education.nh.gov/certification/documents/code_conduct.pdf and the New Hampshire Code of Ethics for Educational Professional is found at https://www.education.nh.gov/news/2018/documents/code-of-ethics-code-of-conduct.pdf

Chapter 3

The Principal as Evaluator

"When principals establish trusting school spaces, serious school improvement and success can occur."[1]

We start this section with the proposition that building-level leadership matters. Principals play a critical role in the academic success of their students. Teachers' general sphere of influence is the classroom while the school is the principal's In particular, principals exercise influence over the academic program by the quality of the teachers they recruit, retain, and remove.[2] "Principals are central figures in schools whose actions directly shape their schools' climate."[3] This influence includes the system and practice of supervision and evaluation of the faculty.

Principals are on the front line of teacher evaluations. Their observations and evaluations have long formed the basis for holding teachers accountable for their professional practice. "In addition to both formal and informal observations of teachers in the classroom, principals receive feedback from students and parents and hear 'water cooler' talk from other teachers."[4] Principals, as part of their leadership responsibilities, occupy a unique position for purposes of evaluation.

The principal's knowledge and skills are central to discharging their responsibility to effectively supervise and evaluate the faculty. Thus, documentation begins at the school level—the seat of a principal's authority and responsibility. Consequently, DiPaola and Hoy assert that the principal is "responsible for the removal of incompetent, ineffective teachers from the profession."[5] The primary objective of a school district's employee evaluation system is the improvement employees' performance so they can become successful and contribute to achieving the district's goals of properly educating its students.

"The district's evaluation system thus serves as a secondary function—the removal of the unsatisfactory employee."[6]

A study by a University of Michigan professor of education policy and a professor of economics, Brian A. Jacobs, found that the primary manner in which principals influence student performance is by affecting the composition, through recruitment and retention, of the teachers in the school.[7] He found that principals are significantly more likely to fire teachers who are frequently absent and who have the worst evaluations in the past.[8] The influence of prior evaluations on dismissal decisions is intuitive with empirical evidence from this study confirming the importance of evaluations. This also indicates that dismissal for incompetence is typically not a single evaluation event. With the exception of egregious conduct, usually involving immorality or felonious criminal behavior, data gathering and analysis takes time to correctly identify the deficiency in order provide a remediation plan.

However, quality supervision and evaluation practices are time intensive, and time has long been the "boogeyman" of educators—"it's always chasing them."[9] A study by researchers Thomas A. Kersten and Marla S. Isreal found that 47 percent of their sample of 102 K-8 school buildings identified time limitations as an impediment to highly effective teacher evaluations.[10] The respondents reported that they were required to evaluate too many teachers and that the paperwork demands associated with the observations and evaluations were extensive.[11]

These data are consistent with the findings from the National Center for Education Statistics *Principal Questionnaire* (7,459 principal respondents), which is part of the *Schools and Staffing Survey* (2007–2008). The respondents answered the prompt: "In your opinion, are the following considered barriers to the dismissal of poor-performing of incompetent teachers in this school?" Almost 38 percent of the respondents checked Yes to "Tight timelines for completing documentation."[12]

Principals are responsible for the efficient functioning of their school. The Vanderbilt Assessment of Leadership in Education identified six key school leadership processes.[13] Principals are the instructional leaders and are often the school law leaders of the school.[14] Teacher evaluation is a significant part of their duties, but not their only duty.[15] The principal faces unique characteristics and challenges making their oversight role more complex than others who might be in management positions in other public or even private settings.

While many eagerly compare schools to business enterprises they are quite different, especially with respect to the roles of managers. Principals, we suggest, are charged with much greater responsibilities and asked to do so with fewer resources. One study notes that "[v]ery few managers in business and other professions are charged with supervising the work of so many employees, let alone taking charge of facilities, public relations, professional development, and miscellaneous tasks such as lunchroom supervision or chaperoning school dances."[16]

For example, Matthew Hicks noted in his doctoral dissertation on high school followership that school principals often are overburdened with the expectations and demands of their work and struggle to accomplish all that is required of them.[17] Furthermore, he asserted, from his review of the literature, that principals have a greater span of control over their personnel than managers in manufacturing and other occupations which impacts their ability to effectively supervise the school's employees.[18] An increased span of control for principals stresses the time that is available for this critical responsibility. Observations and conferences must take place during work time, often forcing the principal to analyze the data and construct a document that fairly reflects the findings. The emphasis on increasing the principal's attention to instruction has created time management problems that affect the principal's already stressed day.

In addition, principal responsibilities involve the sometimes-conflicting roles of supporting and evaluating teachers. DiPaola and Hoy note that "[a]lthough principals may be supportive and helpful to teachers, they also have the burden of making organizational decisions about competence."[19] A principal's supervision of teachers is not only difficult but often lonely and can, sometimes, interfere with their willingness to make tough decisions that might arise from evaluation.

Too often when faced with the stress of confronting and documenting a case for dismissal of an incompetent teacher, the principal goes selectively blind to the behaviors to the detriment of students, the faculty, and the community. Gathering the courage and the skills to sit across from a colleague in your school and tell the truth about the teacher's classroom behaviors is daunting. But to select personal comfort over what your students deserve is unacceptable.

At the minimum, it must be underscored that the evaluation system must be fair, accurate, and conducted in good faith if it is to be a positive and meaningful process that develops, improves, and maintains teaching skills and competencies. A selective blindness will potentially discredit the value of an evaluation system in the eyes of the faculty and, possibly, in the eyes of a third party that may ultimately be asked to rule on an adverse employment decision made by a principal. Of course, with that said, an evaluation must be about more than dismissal and discipline.

If it is only perceived as punitive and not a system infused with fairness built to identify effectiveness, support effectiveness, and build effectiveness, its true value of developing professionals may get lost in the turbulence of discipline and dismissal.[20] Discipline including dismissal may be an outcome of the evaluation, and this high stakes decision requires a knowledgeable, fair evaluator to conduct the evaluation.

A key element in the supervision and evaluation process is the documentation of what has been observed or the facts that have been discovered.[21] The lack of appropriate documentation to support dismissal underscores the importance of proper documentation.[22] An adverse employment decision based on unclear (or lack of) documentation will face scrutiny and, in some instances, be overruled by an objective third party, like a court. For example, in 2011, the New York Supreme Court held, "However, [the teacher] submitted evidence that the principal who made the determination to award the 2008-09 [unsatisfactory rating] did not observe [the teacher's] teaching during either of the final two years at the school."[23]

Similarly, the Supreme Court of Illinois in a 2016, teacher dismissal case, ordered the reinstatement with back pay of a tenured high school math teacher.[24] The teacher had been dismissed for cause, including being late for school while attending to declining health issues of a parent, failure to submit lesson plans, and "generally slow progress" of her first hour of her first period geometry class.[25] The court found that two of the three complaints were not supported "by the weight of the evidence."[26] In other words, the documentation did not support the dismissal.

However, in a contrasting case, a principal developed sufficient evidence through an effective documentation system and the tenacity to place the need for students to have a competent teacher leading their class at the forefront of priorities. A primary teacher had been placed on four improvement plans by three principals while teaching at four different schools in the school district. What has been characterized as the "dance of the lemons" or the "turkey trot" in which incompetent teachers are moved around from school to school, ended with her last principal. The principal placed the teacher on two improvement plans within a three-year period and wrote several letters of reprimand for such actions as using corporal punishment to discipline students and not beginning her class's school day on time.[27]

The principal's ability to document the teacher's performance issue when the matter ultimately reached the courts. Indeed, the Mississippi Court of Appeals held the principal's documentation contained substantial evidence that the teacher was underperforming and failed to meet the requirements of her improvement plan which were designed to improve her instructional skills. The plaintiff teacher failed to provide evidence that her dismissal was arbitrary or capricious.

The reliability and validity of a teacher evaluation system depends upon the skill level of the evaluator. An Ohio study of principal perceptions (N = 50) of the new state Ohio Teacher Evaluation System found:

- 88 percent agree or strongly agree that they "have the skills necessary to complete teacher evaluations effectively"; and

- 72 percent agree or strongly agree that they "have the knowledge necessary to complete teacher evaluations effectively."[28]

However, not all studies support these perceptions. A study of Florida principals found that they felt less effective, only 31 percent felt fully effective, at "releasing or counseling out teachers."[29] These tasks, especially releasing a teacher from employment, involve the skill of proper documentation. Problems must be identified early so that the employee has the ability to remedy the deficiency in a timely manner before the concern about performance is magnified. Importantly, students in classrooms must not be allowed to languish in their classroom with subpar teaching.

In fact, concerns about the principal's efficacy in evaluating and documenting teacher behaviors indicate this as a challenge. For example, Edwin M. Bridges, an early researcher on incompetent teachers, noted over thirty-five years ago three sets of interrelated problems that impact the evaluation of teachers, which seems salient today:

(1) the legal barriers to removing tenured teachers for incompetence in the classroom[30];
(2) the technical problems in measuring teacher effectiveness; and
(3) the human obstacles that are involved, including the willingness and the ability of supervisors to carry out their responsibilities for teacher evaluation, remediation, and dismissal.[31] "Many school administrators, like their counterparts in business and the more prestigious professions, are inclined to tolerate and protect the poor performer."[32]

It is noteworthy that Bridges found the role of the principal to be one of the issues in evaluating teachers. He identified "willingness" and "ability" as key principal dispositions and skills.[33] Consequently, knowledge of proper documentation should improve the principal's concern for "ability" and may influence "willingness" if the principal believes that she or he has a higher skill level.

Research by Connelly, De Mitchell, and Gagnon reviewed a study of principals' perceived barriers to dismissing poor performing or incompetent teachers.[34] They reviewed Public School Principal Questionnaire of the Schools and Staffing Survey (National Center on Education Statistics, 2010). This nationally representative survey is administered by the National Center for Educational Statistics (NCES). Approximately 7,500 principals responded to the survey. Germane to this discussion, the survey found that 67 percent of the responding principals stated that the effort required for documentation was a barrier.[35]

The process of documentation for dismissal "often arouse powerful emotions as fear, self-doubt, anger, and guilt."[36] While principals do bear the "lion's share" of responsibility and work, they should not feel as though they work on an island. Indeed, ultimately, a decision to nonrenew or terminate a teacher will rest in the hands of a superintendent who will make a recommendation to the school board. In other words, superintendents must ensure they are properly supporting their principals as they make difficult decisions that can frequently invite work-place stress. Support from the upper levels of administrations sends a message about the importance of accountability in word and deed on the part of the superintendent and can play an important role in shaping the culture of a school district.

PEER ASSISTANCE AND REVIEW PROGRAMS AND DOCUMENTATION

Principals are tasked with the major responsibility for the supervision and evaluation of teachers. However, a small number of school districts and unions, most notably the American Federal of Teachers (AFT), collaborated with their school district to institute a program, Peer Assistance and Review (PAR), in which selected highly qualified teachers evaluate novice teachers.[37] The AFT first bargained a system of PAR in Toledo, Ohio, in 1981. The National Education Association Foundation in May of 2012 issued a policy brief on PAR. The Brief describes the rationale and structure of PAR programs. However, it does not clearly endorse a position of adoption concluding that it is "powerful [and] worthy of consideration."[38]

PAR programs' focus on working with beginning teachers expanded in a number of school districts to include teachers in need of support. The addition of struggling teachers underscores the relation of PAR to the need for quality documentation. Peer assistance review is not to be confused with mentoring programs. PAR is more than just a buddy system. It was meant to have teeth. While PAR can and does use elements of coaching and non-evaluative support, it has the additional element of evaluation, which sets it apart from mentoring.

PAR is a departure from the typical administrator-driven evaluation system. It invites a shared responsibility for evaluation, with expert consulting teachers not only mentoring but more importantly evaluating novice teachers as well as teachers whose practice has fallen below standards. The traditional approach of administration having the sole responsibility for evaluation and the union holding the administration accountable for a fair process is altered. However, the importance of providing a fair process remains untouched.

In important ways, especially as they relate to documentation, PAR does not change the obligations of supervisors. Because a PAR decision may implicate due process protections, providing documentation "through observation notes, summary reports, and evidence of assistance" remains undisturbed. Similarly, appropriate documentation will be necessary for potential charges brought by the teacher against the union for failing to meet its duty of fair representation.[39]

If anything, PAR may help ensure the integrity of evaluation documentation because principals and others will recognize that their opinions will be scrutinized by others. Without supporting evidence that is documented, the credibility of those opinions may be diminished. Similarly, effective documentation increases that credibility.

PAR programs provide feedback and recommendations designed to improve professional practice. Even though the deliverable is a summative evaluation, it is an evaluation that has high stakes attached to it—retention or dismissal. Whether it is the principal or teacher member of a PAR team,[40] the principles and practices of an effective documentation system well serves their respective responsibilities and the professional development of novice and experienced teachers.

CONCLUDING COMMENTS

Principals have a central role as the instructional and legal leaders of their school to acquire and exercise the necessary skills to fairly document teacher performance with the goal of assisting the teacher in providing a quality educational program for her or his students—a shared goal for the teacher and the principal. The burden is on the school district to prove the case, and this often results in the principal's documentation being part of the hearing/trial. "Without a soundly documented case, the judgment of the supervisor will be severely tested and found wanting."[41]

Therefore, principals who are properly trained, supported, and held accountable for the implementation of effective documentation strategies are necessary for ensuring quality instruction. The supervisor needs skills in documenting teacher behaviors including instruction and teacher-student relations. Skills, will, and support are necessary in order for the principal to discharge an incompetent teacher effectively, efficiently, and fairly.

A principal's level of success in teacher supervision and evaluation depends in part on the level of sophistication with which data is collected and interpreted, his or her investment in time and energy in gathering information, and his or her beliefs, the efficacy of a particular teacher.

Brian A, Jacobs and Lars Lefgren, "Can Principals Identify Effective Teachers? Evidence on Subjective Evaluation in Education" *Journal of Labor Economics* 26 (2008): 101–136, 105.

NOTES

1. Heather E. Price, "Principal-Teacher Interactions: How Affective Relations Shape Principal and Teacher Attitudes" *Educational Administration Quarterly* 48 (2012): 39–85, 42.
2. We focus on the importance of evaluation of teachers and the use of effective documentation approaches and strategies. However, given the importance of recruiting, retaining, and removing ineffective principals, the following short report may be instructive. Sara Sheldon, *Evaluating School Principals: A Legislative Approach* (Denver, CO: National Conference of State Legislatures May 2013).
3. Price, *supra* note 1, at 40.
4. Douglas N. Harris, William K. Ingle, and Stacey A. Rutledge, "How Teacher Evaluation Methods Matter for Accountability: A Comparative Analysis of Teacher Effectiveness Ratings by Principals and Teacher Value-Added Measure." *American Educational Research Journal* 51 (2014): 73–112, 75.
5. Michael F. DiPaola and Wayne K. Hoy, *Principals Improving Instruction: Supervision, Evaluation, and Professional Development* (Boston: Pearson, 2008), 165.
6. Kelly Frels, Janet L. Horton, Lisa McBride, and Ilya Feldsherov, *A Documentation System for Teacher Improvement or Termination* (7th Ed.) (Cleveland, OH: Education Law Association, 2014), 7.
7. Brian A. Jacobs, "Do Principals Fire the Worst Teachers?" *Educational Evaluation and Policy Analysis* 33 (December 2011): 403–34, 404–06.
8. Jacobs, "Do Principals Fire the Worst Teachers?" 429.
9. Denisa R. Superville, "Teacher Evaluations Have Dramatically Changed the Principal's Job." *Education Week* (November 13, 2018). Site visited December 18, 2019, available at https://www.edweek.org/ew/articles/2018/11/14/teacher-evaluations-have-dramatically-changed-the-principals.html (quoting the president of the National Association of Elementary School Principals regarding the boogeyman, "Although there have been some real positives that have come from the teacher evaluation [reforms], that boogeyman has gotten much larger.").
10. Thomas A. Kersten and Marla S. Isreal, "Teacher Evaluation: Principals' Insights and Suggestions for Improvement." *Planning and Change* 36 (2005): 47–67, 47.
11. Kersten and Isreal, "Teacher Evaluation," 57. Time was the largest impediment followed by unions and school culture, with the actual evaluation system as third impediment. Ibid., 61.
12. Vincent J. Connelly, Todd A. DeMitchell, and Douglas Gagnon, "Teacher Evaluation: Principal Perceptions of the Barriers to Dismissal Research, Policy, and Practice." *Education Law & Policy Review* 1 (2014): 172–192, 183.
13. Author, *Perspective. Assessing the Effectiveness of School Leaders: New Directions and Processes* (New York: The Wallace Foundation, March 2009), 9 (citing Planning, Implementing, supporting, advocating, Communicating, and Monitoring as key leadership processes). Site visited April 10, 2019, available at https://www.wallacefoundation.org/knowledge-center/Documents/Assessing-the-Effectiveness-of-School-Leaders.pdf.
14. For a discussion of principals as the legal leaders of their school, see David Schimmel, Suzanne Eckes, and Matthew Militello, *Principals Teaching the Law: 10 Legal Lessons Your Teachers Must Know* (Thousand Oaks, CA: Corwin, 2010).

15. Rick DuFour and Mike Mattos, "How Do Principals Really Improve Schools." *Educational Leadership* 70 (April 2013): 34–40, 36 (recognizing the "crushing demands on the contemporary principal" which requires attention to at least twenty-one different demands principals must address).

16. Author, *Perspectives from Accomplished California Teachers. A Quality Teacher in Every Classroom: Creating a Teacher Evaluation System that Works for California* (Stanford, CA: National Board Resource Center, 2010), 3. Site visited May 2, 2019, available at https://edpolicy.stanford.edu/sites/default/files/publicatio ns/quality-teacher-every-classroom-evaluation-system-works-california.pdf. The report recommends that a new evaluation system be designed around the following principles:

1. Teacher evaluation should be based on professional standards.
2. Teacher evaluation should include performance assessments.
3. The design of a new evaluation system should build on successful, innovative practices.
4. Evaluations should consider teacher practice and performance, as well as an array of student outcomes for teams of teachers as well as individual teachers.
5. Evaluations should be frequent and conducted by expert evaluators.
6. Evaluation leading to teacher tenure must be more intensive.
7. Evaluation should be accompanied by useful feedback, connected to professional development opportunities, and reviewed by evaluation teams.

17. Matthew S. Hicks, *An Exploratory Mixed-Methods Study of Followership Types in New Hampshire High School* (unpublished doctoral dissertation, PhD) (Durham, NH: University of New Hampshire, 2018), 16.

18. Hicks, *An Exploratory Mixed-Methods Study*.

19. DiPaola, *supra* note 5, 24.

20. For a discussion of using professional development strategies to improve teaching performance as opposed to just firing teachers, see Craig D. Gerald, *Movin' It and Improvin' It! Using Both Education Strategies to Increase Teaching Effectiveness* (Washington, DC: Center for American Progress, January 2012). Site visited May 2, 2019, available at https://www.issuelab.org/resources/12399/12399.pdf.

21. See *Spencer-East Brookfield Regional Sch. Dist. v. Spencer-East Brookfield Teachers' Assoc.*, 101 N.E.3d 305, 308 (Mass. App. Ct. 2018) (writing, "Such a teacher also has the statutory right to receive documentation of the reasons sufficient to allow the teacher to respond.").

22. See Lawrence F. Rossow and Laural Logan-Fain, *The Law of Teacher Evaluation* (3rd Ed.) (Dayton, OH: Education Law Association, 2013), 17 (writing "it is important for school authorities to have developed a record of the lack of teacher performance in order to dismiss.").

23. *Kolmel v. City of New York*, 930 N.Y.S.2d 573, 574 (A.D. 1 Dept. 2011).

24. *Beggs v. Board. of Education of Murphysboro Community Unit School District*, 72 N.E.3d 288 (2016).

25. Ibid., 293.

26. Ibid., 309. The court found that the third charge was supported but was minor in nature.

27. *Ekanem v. Greenville Public School*, 235 S0. 3d 1431, 1433 (Miss. App. 2017).

28. Theodore J. Kowalski and David Alan Dolph, "Principal Dispositions Regarding the Ohio Teacher Evaluation System." *AASA Journal of Scholarship and Practice* 11 (2015): 1–20, 10. Site visited April 28, 2019, available at https://pdfs.semanticscholar.org/205f/69bd2df90e3d2973976588a13399ef76c50c.pdf?_ga=2.43456933.1658901693.1560260987-590574513.1560260987.

29. Jason A, Grissom and Suzanna Loeb, *Triangulating Principal Effectiveness: How Perspectives of Parents, Teachers, and Assistant Principals Identify the Central Importance of Managerial Skills* (Working Paper 35) (Washington, DC: National Center for Analysis of Longitudinal Data of Education Sciences, December 2009), 16. Site visited April 26, 2019, available at https://www.urban.org/sites/default/files/publication/33316/1001443-Triangulating-Principal-Effectiveness-How-Perspectives-of-Parents-Teachers-and-Assistant-Principals-Identify-the-Central-Importance-of-Managerial-Skills.PDF.

30. Noted education law scholar Perry A. Zirkel addressing the concern about the legal barriers to evaluation that educational leaders confront found that court decisions skew toward the school district. He writes, "In distinguishing the law of teacher evaluation from the lore of teacher evaluation, school officials should use the wide gap as a liberating opportunity for the exercise of professional discretion based on pursuit of excellence rather than fear of litigation." Perry A. Zirkel, *Case Law for Performance Evaluation of Public School Professional Personnel: An Update*, 314 Educ. Law Rep. 1, 1 (2015).

31. Edwin M. Bridges with the assistance of Barry Groves, *Managing the Incompetent Teacher* (Eugene, OR, University of Oregon: Clearinghouse on Educational Management, 1984), 2.

32. Edwin M. Bridges, *The Incompetent Teacher: Managerial Responses* (Philadelphia: The Falmer Press, 1992), 20. "Moreover, the most common response to [incompetence] in all professions, organizations, and societies is to tolerate and protect the inept." Bridges, *The Incompetent Teacher*, 19.

33. Ibid., 25, writing, "Individuals are predisposed to avoid unpleasantness in social encounters. They prefer to be spared the emotional ordeal entailed in criticizing and finding fault with the behaviors of others."

34. Connelly, et al., *supra* note 12 at 172.

35. Ibid., 183. Tenure was the highest named barrier (70.8 percent) followed by documentation (67 percent), with teacher associations or unions the third highest perceived barrier (62.7 percent). Tight timelines for completing documentation (35.8 percent) and dismissal is too stressful and/or uncomfortable (14.6 percent). *Id.* A Spearman Rank Order Correlation between documentation and time for completion of documentation is strong (r_s=5.48). *Id.* at 189. The low rating of stress negatively influencing dismissal strikes as low. Our experience is that there is stress related to confronting an individual about the high stakes of potential dismissal. However, we agree with Professor Meuney that as stressful as it may be the alternative of "keeping an incompetent teacher in the classroom is sure to be more frustrating." (Brendan P. Menuey, "Teachers' Perceptions of Professional Incompetence and Barriers to Dismissal." *Journal of Personnel Evaluation in Education* 18 (2005): 309–325, 309.)

36. Bridges, *supra* 32 at 57.

37. See Author, *Peer Assistance and Review* (Washington, DC: American Federation of Teachers, n.d.). Site visited June 9, 2019 available at https://www.aft.org/position/peer-assistance-and-review. The AFT, noting the needs of beginning teachers, offered the following rationale for PAR programs, "As financially strapped school districts waste money on the endless cycle of recruiting, training and replacing new teachers, the education of students suffers from the faculty turnover. Further, under the current system, tenure decisions are often made on the fly, by ill-prepared principals without the time or the expertise to make informed judgments."

38. Harriet Sanford, *Peer Assistance Review* (NEA Foundation Issue Brief) (Washington, D.C.: NEA Foundation, May 2012). Site visited June 9, 2019, available at https://www.neafoundation.org/wp-content/uploads/2017/06/parfinal-4.pdf.

39. Susan Moore Johnson, John P. Papy, Sarah E. Fiarman, Mindy Sick Munger, and Emily Kalejs Quazilbash, *Teacher to Teacher: Realizing the Potential of Peer Assistance and Review* (Washington, DC: Center for American Progress, May 2010), 19. For a discussion of teachers who believe that PAR has been used as a target against older and minority teachers, see Labor Video Project, "The Fight Against PAR, the Attack on Teachers and Worker Rights with Educator Brian Crowell." *East Bay*, May 17, 2019. Site visited June 11, 2019, available at https://www.indybay.org/newsitems/2019/05/17/18823483.php.

40. For a study of teachers' perceptions of their participation and the central role of principals in a PAR program, see Jennifer Goldstein, "Making Sense of Distributed Leadership: The Case of Peer Assistance Review." *Educational Evaluation and Policy Analysis* 25 (2003): 397–421.

41. Edwin M. Bridges, with the assistance of Barry Groves, *Managing the Incompetent Teacher* (2nd Ed.) (Eugene, OR: Clearinghouse on Educational Management College of Education University of Oregon 1990), 8. Visited June 7, 2019, available at https://pdfs.semanticscholar.org/8ec8/014eb406c1b58f33d2c02e9d37287a356830.pdf.

Chapter 4

Legal Frameworks

Infusing the Evaluation with Fairness

> To a large extent, due process is an exercise in applied ethics: justice is, in the long run, intended to be fairness.[1]

We explored the responsibilities of the principal in the last section. In this chapter, we situate those responsibilities within the legal framework within which the principal must act. We start with due process as the constitutional foundation that defines the rights of the employee and the responsibilities of the employer in using fair laws and a fair process to make employment decisions.

The landscape of teacher evaluation and dismissal are filled with legal requirements and pitfalls for the unwary principal who does not have a basic knowledge of the law—the U.S. Constitution, state statutes, board policies, and collective bargaining agreements (CBA), for example. First, we address the question of what is due process.

WHAT IS DUE PROCESS?

Knowledge of an effective documentation system utilizing legally defensible memoranda for employees in need of improvement is one tool that can be used that protects legitimate employee due process rights and assists in improving the delivery of professional services to students. While the words "due process" may strike fear in some administrators, it should actually inspire a sense of relief for those administrators who are fair and employing a system of documentation that reflects their judgment and what has transpired in a given situation. Fundamentally, due process is about fairness.

An early Illinois Supreme Court decision held that tenure is designed to "improve the [school] system by assuring teachers of experience and ability a continuous service. . . based upon merit and by protecting them against dismissal for reasons that are political, partisan or capricious."[2] Professor McNeal further elaborates on the purpose for tenure writing, "[I]deally, tenure is intended to provide a degree of permanency, stability, and high level of expertise within the teaching force from which students ultimately benefit."[3] Tenure and its attendant due process rights serve the public good. We think most, if not all, principals would agree that a process that ensures fairness and serves the public good is a good thing.

Due process has a long history. It is rooted in common law running back to the Magna Carta in 1215. Its seeds are found in Article 39 of the Magna Carta (or Great Charter), which states, "No freemen shall be taken or imprisoned or disseised or exiled or in any way destroyed, nor will we go upon him nor send upon him, except by the lawful judgment of his peers or by the law of the law."[4] Essentially, the Magna Carta sought protection from a single strong person who could decide the fate of an individual, or government untethered from any restraint.

Tacitly following the lead of the Magna Carta, the U.S. Supreme Court opined, "The touchstone of due process is the protection of the individual against the arbitrary action of government."[5] It provides a process when the employee has a recognized property or liberty right in which that right cannot be taken away by the government without the due process of law. Due process is found in both the Fifth and the Fourteenth Amendments. The Fourteenth Amendment reads in pertinent part, "nor shall any state deprive any person of life, liberty or property."[6]

When teachers receive tenure under the applicable state law, they gain "a legitimate claim" of property[7] and thus are entitled to due process protection when their property (employment) may be taken away.[8] Tenure becomes property in that there is a continuing expectation of employment.[9] It is not a job guarantee, nor a lifetime appointment. It is a fallacy and lore that tenure should be equated as a "job for life." Both teachers and principals who operate under that assumption do so at their peril. Instead, tenure assures that school leaders must demonstrate just cause for termination through the application of due process.

Liberty interests are triggered when the dismissal or nonrenewal implicates a fundamental interest such as free speech. Likewise, if the adverse action stigmatizes or damages the reputation of the employee to such a degree that it harms the future employability of the employee, a teacher can claim their liberty interest has been implicated. Employees asserting a liberty interest violation typically seek a name-clearing hearing. The U.S. Supreme Court in *Paul v. Davis* writes, "Where a person's good name, reputation, honor, or integrity is at stake because of what government is doing to him[/her], notice and opportunity to be heard are essential."[10] However, there must be more than damage to a reputation, there must be a change to the person's legal status—stigma plus.

The Seventh Circuit describes its test on what the plaintiff must prove when asserting a liberty issue. The discharged state employee must show that the public statement(s) of a government official that (1) she or he was stigmatized by the defendant's conduct, (2) the stigmatizing information was publicly disclosed, and (3) the plaintiff "suffered a tangible loss of other employment opportunities as a result of public disclosure."[11] Thus, it is important to remember that in dealing with evaluations (and documentations) that may lead to an adverse employment decision, principals are dealing with sensitive personnel issues and should act accordingly.

WHAT PROCESS IS DUE?

Essentially, due process requires fundamental fairness, thus protecting individuals from the abuse of power and erroneous decisions made by government officials. Boiled down to its core, due process requires government to implement fair laws in a fair manner if it's action infringes upon a person's life liberty, or property. A Texas federal district court in a teacher evaluation case wrote in 2017, "In short, due process is designed to foster government decision-making that is both fair and accurate."[12]

The U.S. Supreme Court in *Morrissey v. Brewer* opined, "Once it is determined that due process applies, the question remains what process is due."[13] The process remains flexible responding to the demands of the particular situation[14]; it is not a "technical concept[] with fixed content."[15] However, there are two elements that comprise due process—procedural due process and substantive due process—which are guaranteed in the U.S. Constitution's Fifth and Fourteenth Amendments. However, it must be remembered that due process rights do not shield the incapable and the incompetent from termination.

Procedural due process guarantees that a person who is deprived of her or his life, liberty, or property is entitled to a fair process. The procedures for possibly taking away a person's life, liberty, or property must meet the requirements of a fair notice and a fair hearing. The notice must contain specific information about the day, time, and place of the hearing. It must also include, with sufficient specificity, notice of the charges against the person so that he or she can prepare an adequate defense.[16]

The U.S. Supreme Court, in a non-education case, held that a proper notice must be "reasonably calculated, under all the circumstances, to apprise interested parties of the pendency of the action and afford them an opportunity to present their objections."[17] Essentially, the fundamental requirement is to provide the opportunity to be heard "at a meaningful time and in a meaningful manner."[18]

An application of notice is a warning letter issued prior to dismissal. A Missouri Court of Appeals overturned a dismissal decision stating in pertinent part that the warning letter was "totally insufficient."[19] The statement of areas that need improvement were so broadly worded—"(1) relationship with students, (2) enthusiasm in teaching, (3) disciplinary policies, and (4) relationship with parents"[20]—that the teacher would not know which conduct was insufficient and what needs to be done to correct the deficiencies.

There was no reasonable assurance that any course of action could be successful. The court stated, "The teacher finds herself in a position of struggling blindly towards undefined and unknown standards of conduct."[21] The warning letter did not comport with statutory requirements of "specifying with particularity," and thus could not constitute a termination notice as required by state law, thus the dismissal proceeding could not commence. The teacher was reinstated to her position with payment of all lost wages.

The hearing must be held before a neutral tribunal with authority in the matter.[22] It must be an orderly proceeding, with the person being charged having the opportunity to review the evidence and to rebut the evidence and most often having the opportunity to cross-examine witnesses.[23] The hearing, except in the matter of exigency of immediate harm, must be held prior to the implementation of discipline.[24] Notice precedes hearing, consequently investigation, process of documenting behavior, is a necessary portion of deciding whether to give notice of charges requiring a hearing.[25] Procedural due process is "tailored" according to the extent of the deprivation a person may suffer at the hands of the government.[26] In other words, the greater the deprivation, the greater the procedural protections.[27]

Substantive due process is concerned with the substance of the law rule or regulation. It ensures "some minimal level of fairness and logic" protecting teachers "from arbitrary, capricious, and insufficiently substantiated deprivations of property, even if all the correct procedures are followed."[28] The law, rule, or regulation that deprives an individual of life, liberty, or property must be reasonable and consistent with the American sense of fairness. It must be clearly and rationally related to a lawful state function (unless the issue involves a fundamental interest and education has not been declared a federal constitutional fundamental interest[29]).

The reasonable person test is used when the issue involves substantive due process. The test asks: "Would a reasonable person understand what to do or not do after reading the law, rule, or regulation?" For example, an Illinois federal district court judge discussed the vagueness doctrine in a student discipline case when he violated the school's loitering rule. Judge Norgle wrote,

If people of common intelligence must guess at an enactment's meaning and differ as to its application, the law is unconstitutionally vague and is void. Accordingly, an enactment must define the prohibited conduct with sufficient definiteness such that an ordinary individual understands just what conduct is prohibited and must define the prohibited conduct in a manner discouraging arbitrary and discriminatory enforcement.[30]

Substantive due process challenges involve questions of vagueness or overbreadth as well as questions about fundamental fairness (conscious shocking behavior[31]). Conscious shocking behavior typically involves an extreme lack of proportionality between the behavior and the discipline. In addition to vagueness requiring knowledge of the law, rule, or regulation, it also discourages its arbitrary or discriminatory enforcement.

For example, a New York teacher sought to have his termination supported by a hearing officer and the Supreme Court, New York County. The teacher argued that his punishment of dismissal "was so disproportionate to the offenses as to be shocking to the court's sense of fairness."[32] The court found that the termination did not shock the conscious. The attempts, lasting two to three years, to assist the teacher to improve his teaching techniques were largely unsuccessful. The fact that the teacher did not believe that his teaching was deficient was noted by the court.

Knowledge of due process protections of a fair process using fair laws is important in providing structure building documentation to be used in any adverse employment decision. Anchoring documentation to fairness helps to ensure that the employee's due process rights are being respected and protected. It also builds confidence in the system.

PROGRESSIVE DISCIPLINE AND JUST CAUSE

Bob Chase, President of the National Education Association (February 5, 1997).

The fact that while the majority of teachers are capable and dedicated—professionals who put children's interests first—there are indeed some bad teachers in America's schools. And it is *our* job as a union to improve these teachers or—that failing—to get them out of the classroom.[33]

Progressive discipline is exactly what it sounds like: it calls upon an employer to use various degrees of discipline before termination.[34] It is, if you will, a "sliding scale" of discipline with the final step as termination The premise is that employees should have an opportunity to remediate their behavior before termination. The focus is on rehabilitation and preventing termination and discipline "small" transgressions (e.g., a first instance of being late to bus duty) should match the degree of the infraction.

Progressive discipline is embedded in "just cause." For instance, the first inquiry in a just cause analysis requires an arbitrator to determine if the employer gave the employee sufficient notice that their behavior jeopardizes their job. Of course, in certain egregious circumstances, an employer can terminate without progressive discipline.

A district's discipline of an employee covered by a CBA must be supported by "just cause." Most CBA contain a "just cause" requirement and, even where cannot be found within the agreement, arbitrators will generally impose one. Essentially just cause asks whether the conduct justified discipline and was just/fair—would a reasonable person have made this decision based on what is morally right and fair? Just cause, as commonly used, consists of seven tests. Arbitrator Carroll R. Daugherty defined the tests for just cause in the following way:

(1) Did the company give the employee forewarning or foreknowledge of the possible or probable disciplinary consequences of the employee's conduct?
(2) Was the company's rule or managerial order reasonably related to (a) the orderly, efficient, and safe operation of the company's business and (b) the performance that the company might properly expect of the employee?
(3) Did the company, before administering discipline to an employee, make an effort to discover whether the employee did in fact violate or disobey a rule or order of management?
(4) Was the company's investigation conducted fairly and objectively?
(5) At the investigation did the "judge" obtain substantial evidence or proof that the employee was guilty as charged?
(6) Has the company applied its rules, orders, and penalties evenhandedly and without discrimination to all employees?
(7) Was the degree of discipline administered by the company in a particular case reasonably related to (a) the seriousness of the employee's proven offense and (b) the record of the employee in his service with the company?[35]

To some, the principles set forth above may seem onerous. Yet it is important to remember that in the context of a challenge to a dismissal (or some discipline), a third-party neutral (such as an arbitrator) will review these questions to determine if "just cause" existed in a given situation. Thus, the importance of these tests cannot be understated and that importance only increases as the stakes get higher when a discipline decision is challenged.

DISMISSAL AND NONRENEWAL

As discussed above, due process is required for an adverse employment decision that implicates an employee's life, liberty, or property interests. Tenure confers property because it constitutes a continuing expectation that is conferred upon the employee; it is not a subject expectation on the part of the employee. A non-tenured teacher does not have a continuing expectation beyond the end of the contract period.

The dismissal of a tenured teacher requires a notice and a hearing in which the affected employee has the opportunity to hear and respond to the cause that supports the dismissal. A non-tenured teacher, essentially a teacher without a property right, is not entitled to hearing. However, that employee is entitled to a hearing when his or her liberty interests have allegedly been abridged by the employing school district. It is also important to note that while a non-tenured teacher does not have a property interest (entitling them to notice and due process), they retain protections that might arise under other bodies of law, such as a CBA, the Constitution, or Civil Rights protections (e.g., protection from adverse employment decisions based on race, gender, etc.).

The exceptions to this general rule of probationary (non-tenured) teachers not being accorded a hearing maybe found in either state law or when the employee is facing a dismissal during the life of the contract. In other words, a teacher who is being dismissed in November has a continuing expectation of employment up to the end of the contract at the end of the school year. Therefore, the teacher is entitled to a hearing because of the potential loss of property.

Administrators must be aware of the statutory and school district timelines and procedures. For example, if state law requires that a non-tenured teacher must receive a nonrenewal notice by April 15, the employee must receive the notice in accordance with the stated deadline. Failure to meet this deadline most often results in the teacher being retained for the following year. An argument that the process started prior to April 15 is not successful. Consequently, school administrators must meet the deadline. The courts in this situation do not look upon substantial compliance favorably; full compliance with a deadline is required.

AN INDUCED EXIT[36]

Sometimes a school district will negotiate a resignation of a teacher in exchange for not pursuing disciplinary action, usually dismissal or nonrenewal of the teaching contract. The process of inducing an exit takes place before the dismissal decision and is a negotiation process. The goal is to avoid a dismissal proceeding and to reach a settlement for separation. It provides a face-saving strategy in that the teacher can claim a voluntary exit from the school district. A dismissal is not only potentially stigmatizing; it is highly stressful. For the administration, the cost in terms of time and money is avoided. Neither of these are trivial reasons for pursuing a negotiated exit. While some may criticize them as "pay-outs," they are often used in the private sector for the very same reasons.

Sometimes these negotiations constitute confidential settlement protections.[37] The inducement to resign may include continued health care insurance for a specified time. It may include the use of unused sick leave with the educator taking the leave immediately. The high school example at the beginning of the section used this approach. The cost to the school for the use of sick leave was balanced against bringing in a competent teacher right away in order to salvage some learning time for the students.

Sometimes it involves writing a neutral letter of recommendation. This option is one to carefully approach. The school district does not want to write a letter that obscures the problematic professional behavior of the employee. It does not want to be a party to foisting on an unsuspecting school and its students a problem. In the case cited above, the high school teacher was not offered a letter of recommendation. School officials must not continue the practice commonly known as "passing the trash," "the turkey trot," or the "dance of the lemons."

An issue that sometimes arises in a resignation letter in exchange for dropping the disciplinary proceeding is, can a teacher withdraw a retirement agreement in exchange for discontinuing the disciplinary hearing? A New York teacher signed an agreement to "irrevocably retire for employment" and the school district would not take further disciplinary action against the teacher. The teacher, his attorney, and the school district's attorney signed the agreement. The stipulation had a line for the superintendent's signature. Before the superintendent signed the agreement, the teacher notified the school district that he changed his mind and wanted to rescind the agreement. The district said no.

The teacher went to court arguing that the stipulation was unenforceable because not all parties had signed the document before he withdrew it. The Supreme Court, Appellate Division found this argument "unavailing." The court stated that the plaintiff teacher failed to show "the existence of fraud, collusion, mistake, accident, or that the counsel lacked the [school board's] consent."[38] The school district's counsel, the court found, acted on behalf of the school district, thus his signature constitutes a binding contract. Plaintiff's agreement to retire was irrevocable and he understood its consequences.

CONCLUDING THOUGHTS ON THE APPROACH OF THE PRINCIPAL

Even if a probationary teacher is not entitled to due process in a nonrenewal decision, fairness must still pervade the evaluation process and be the touchstone for the principal. A teacher should not go through an entire year and not have a good sense of the outcome of the summative evaluation. Failure to work with employees identifying strengths and weaknesses for improvement with a focus on developing and retaining quality teachers must not be the principal's standard of practice. The culture of a school and the value ascribed to its teachers and staff is heavily influenced by the way in which the principal supervises and evaluates.

Many principals and administrators operate under a dangerous fallacy. Indeed, with respect to non-tenured or probationary teachers, principals or administrators have often been heard to say: "I can terminate or non-renew a non-tenured teacher without any reason." Unfortunately, as we have noted above, nothing could be further from the truth. First, as a matter of best practice and ethics, a principal should always have reasons for nonrenewing a teacher and the teacher should be aware of those reasons. Second, as a legal matter, a principal should always have reasons—well-documented ones, in fact—supporting a decision to nonrenew *any* teacher, including those without tenure.

As we advise above, and it is worth repeating here, non-tenured teachers enjoy protections from a host of other laws, such as anti-discrimination laws like the Age Discrimination in Employment Act (the ADEA) which protects employees over the age of forty from being terminated because of their age. We advise that the mistaken phrase of principal-lore ought best to be reframed as follows: A principal terminating or nonrenewing an employee should always have reasons—and they should be well documented.

In sum, the power that a principal wields when it comes to evaluations is substantial not only for the teacher but for the school, its students, and its community. The actions of the principal on critical issues communicate the values of the school. What the professional expectations are in our school are communicated by the principal. Can I trust the principal to be fair? Principals who demonstrate the skill and will to ensure quality professional practice in their school support an effective education for the community's children.

From the very beginning, our state and national constitutions and laws have laid great emphasis on procedural and substantive safeguards designed to assure fair trials before impartial tribunals in which every defendant stands equal before the law.
  Gideon v. Wainwright, 372 U.S. 335, 344 (1963).

NOTES

1. Michael Scriven, "Due Process in Adverse Personnel Action" *Journal of Personnel Evaluation in Education* 11 (1997): 127-137, 128.
2. *Donahoo v. Board of Education*, 109 N.E. 2d 787, 789 (Ill. 1952).
3. Laura McNeal, "Total Recall: The Rise and Fall of Teacher Tenure." *Hofstra Labor & Employment Law Journal* 30 (2013): 489–510, 491.
4. Author, "Part I: What Is the Rule of Law." *American Bar Association Division for Public Education* (n.d.), 4. Site visited on April 28, 2019, available at https://www.americanbar.org/content/dam/aba/migrated/publiced/features/Part1DialogueROL.authcheckdam.pdf.
5. *County of Sacramento v. Lewis*, 523 U.S. 833, 845 (1998) quoting *Wolff v. McDonnell*, 418 U.S. 539, 558 (1974).
6. U.S. AMEND. XIV, § 1.
7. *Board of Regents v. Roth*, 408, U.S. 564, 576 (1972). (further writing, as opposed to an "abstract need or desire for it . . . [or] a unilateral expectation of it."). Ibid.
8. *Cleveland Board of Education. v. Loudermill*, 470 U.S. 532, 546–548 (1985).
9. For a discussion of due process and critiques of tenure, Todd A. DeMitchell and Joseph J. Onosko, "*Vergara v. State of California:* The End of Tenure or a Flawed Ruling." *Southern California Interdisciplinary Law Journal* 25 (2016): 589 S. CAL. INTERDIS. L. J. 589–624, 593–602 (2016).
10. *Paul v. Davis*, 424 U.S. 693, 711 (1976).
11. *Hamerski v. Belleville Area Special Services Cooperative*, 302 F.Supp. 3d 992, 1001 (S.D. Ill. 2018).
12. *Houston Federation of Teachers, Local 2415 v. Houston Independent. School District*, 251 F. Supp. 3d 1168, 1176 (S.D. Tex. 2017) (quoting *Carey v. Piphus*, 435 U.S. 247, 262 (1978).
13. *Morrissey v. Brewer*, 408 U.S. 471, 481 (1972).
14. Ibid.
15. *Cafeteria Workers v. McElroy*, 367 U.S. 886, 895 (1961).
16. *See Griggsville-Perry School District*, 127 LA 1542 (2010) (asserting that a discharge notice that stated that the employee "did not relate well" to students and "was not always pleasant" failed to provide proper notice for the preparation of an adequate defense).
17. *Mullane v. Central Hanover Bank & Trust Co.*, 339 U.S. 306, 314 (1950).
18. *Armstrong v. Manzo*, 380 U.S. 545, 552 (1965).
19. *Pollard v. Board of Education Reorganized School District No. III*, 533 S.W. 2d 667, 670 (Mo. Ct. App. 1976).
20. Ibid.
21. Ibid.
22. School boards and boards of trustees are presumed to be impartial. The plaintiff carries the burden of proving otherwise. *Hortonville Joint School District No. 1 v. Hortonville Education Association*, 426 U.S. 482 (1976). However, if the school board is the adjudicator of the dismissal hearing, it must maintain distance from the administration, which is bringing the case for dismissal. If a school law attorney is

involved in the process, she or he must either advise the administration or the school board and not both. Failure to heed this may result in a finding that the teacher's right to a fair hearing has been violated.

23. A recent controversy regarding cross-examination has arisen in Title IX sexual assault cases when the accused student asserts a right to cross-exam the accuser. Two cases out of the Sixth Circuit Court of Appeals upheld the right under due process of the respondent to have some form of cross-examination; see Richard Fossey and Todd A. DeMitchell, *"Doe v. Baum*: The Sixth Circuit Reiterates that Students Accused of Sexual Assault Are Constitutionally Entitled to Confront Their Accusers at University Title IX Disciplinary Hearings." *School Law Reporter* 60 (December 2018): 189–191 (Cleveland, OH: Education Law Association). The Appellate Court in *Doe v. Baum*, 903 F.3d 575 (6th Cir. 2018), wrote that cross-examination "is the greatest legal engine ever invented for uncovering the truth," allowing the accused to identify inconsistencies as well as giving the "fact-finder an opportunity to assess a witness's demeanor and determine who may be trusted." Ibid., 581.

24. See *Cleveland v. Board of Education v. Loudermill*, 470 U.S. at 544 (asserting that due process requires a pre-termination hearing regarding termination, specifically the right to respond to the charges supporting the dismissal).

25. See *Fritz v. Evers*, 907 F.3d 533, 534 (7th Cir. 2018) (asserting, "Administrative investigations likewise precede hearings.").

26. *Goldberg v. Kelly*, 397 U.S. 254, 268–269 (1970) (footnote omitted).

27. See *Hagar v. Reclamation District* 111 U.S. 701, 708 (1884) (asserting, "Due process of law is [a process which], following the forms of law, is appropriate to the case and just to the parties affected. It must be pursued in the ordinary mode prescribed by law; it must be adapted to the end to be attained and whenever necessary to the protection of the parties, it must give them an opportunity to be heard respecting the justice of the judgment sought.")

28. Derek W. Black, "The Constitutional Challenge to Teacher Tenure." *California Law Review* 104 (2016): 75–148, 103–104.

29. See *San Antonio Independent School District, v. Rodriguez*, 411 U.S. 1, 38 (1973) (writing, "We have carefully considered each of the arguments supportive of the District Court's finding that education is a fundamental right or liberty and have found those arguments unpersuasive.").

30. *Wiemerslage v. Maine Township High School District 207*, 824 F. Supp. 136, 139–140 (N.D. Ill. 1993). The rule prohibiting loitering in the Hamlin Gates Area had sufficient clarity for the plaintiff to know that standing in the area instead of proceeding through it violates the rule.

31. See *Rochin v. California*, 342 U.S. 165, 169 (1972), (holding that substantive due process is violated when government, public school, conduct "offend[s] those canons of decency and fairness." In other words, a "sense of justice" (at 173) must not "shock the conscience" (at 172). Similarly, due process is violated when government conduct reaches "a demonstrable level of outrageousness." *Hampton v. United States*, 425 U.S. 484, 495 n.7 (1976).

32. *Ferraro v. Farina*, 69 N.Y.S. 3d 266, 267 (A.D. 1 Dept. 2017).

33. Bob Chase, *Reinventing Unions for a New Era. Remarks before the National Press Club*, National Education Association (February 5, 1997): 1–7, 3. Site visited

on June 14, 2019, available at http://www.eiaonline.com/ChaseNewUnionism1997.pdf. Furthermore, he states, "Quality must begin at home, within our own ranks. If a teacher is not measuring up in the classroom, to put it boldly, if there is a bad teacher in one of our schools, then we must do something about it." Ibid., 5.

34. *American Jurisprudence 2d* § 43 (2012) defining progressive discipline as requiring "a series of warnings and attempts to correct behavior prior to discipline or which require different types of discipline in response to different degrees of misconduct, ranging from reprimand to discharge." (citations omitted).

35. Enterprise Wire Company and Enterprise Independent Union, 46 LA 359 (1964).

36. Induced exit is a term used by Edwin M. Bridges (*The Incompetent Teacher: Managerial Responses* (Philadelphia: The Falmer Press, 1992)).

37. For a discussion of the controversy over public access to confidential employment settlement agreements, see Mark A. Paige, "Too Much Sun Can Burn: Reassessing Public Access to Confidential Employment Settlement Agreements in Public Education," *Albany Law Review* 82 (2018): 379–406. Professor Paige phrases the tension in the following way:

> The task, then, is to balance between competing policy goals of transparency (that, again, have theoretical benefits) and of encouraging settlement agreements (which has demonstrable value to public entities and taxpayers).
>
> Paige, "Too Much Sun Can Burn," 382.

38. *Nobile v. Board of Education of the City School District of the City of New York*, 89 N.Y.S. 3d 137, 138 (A.D. 1 Dept. 2018).

Chapter 5

The Five Fatal "Eyes" of Unprofessional Conduct

The dismissal of a public school teacher is usually governed by the law of the state in which the teacher is employed. The charges and the documentation providing a preponderance of evidence to support the dismissal must comport with those laws. While the specific causes may vary from state to state,[1] We believe that the following discussion of the "Eyes" of Unprofessional Conduct may provide a perspective that may generalize across the nation's public school systems. To be sure, every case is different and every case requires that principals have facts to support an adverse employment decision. Nevertheless, we suggest that the incidents that you encounter in practice likely fall within one, or more, of the Fatal "Eyes" noted below.

PROFESSIONAL CODES OF ETHICS

The many aspects of the work of the teacher are grounded in the status of the teacher as a professional. A profession is distinguished from a trade. It comprises a group of individuals who organize their work "to support a moral ideal."[2] Professional work is complex and non-routine. Professions are built on a specialized body of knowledge usually gained through extensive education and training, exercised in the best interests of the person receiving the service. Linda Darling-Hammond, noted teacher policy expert, states that professionalism is predicated upon three principles:

1. Knowledge is the basis for permission to practice and for decisions that are made with respect to the unique needs of clients.
2. The practitioner pledges his[/her] first concern to the welfare of the client.

3. The profession assumes collective responsibility for the definition, transmittal, and enforcement of professional standards of practice and ethics.[3]

It involves a standard of practice recognized and adhered to by the practitioners. These standards are recognized accepted by the profession. The standards are enforced by the professional organization, typically through an internal code of ethics. "Professional codes of ethics represent a consensus of the normative values, beliefs, and concerns about appropriate behavior."[4] The code of ethics supports the commitment to serve the public and serves as a balance to professional autonomy.

Professionals who violate their code of conduct can be sanctioned, including disbarment from the practice of law or the loss of the license to practice medicine. For example, the American Bar Association's Model Rules of Professional Conduct: Maintaining the Integrity of the Profession Rule 8.4 Misconduct lists the reasons for professional misconduct for which lawyers are subject to discipline.[5] Similarly, the American Medical Association's Code of Medical Ethics Preamble states, "The following Principles adopted by the American Medical Association are not laws, but standards of conduct that define the essentials of honorable behavior for the physician."[6]

Both of these examples from law and medicine seek to maintain the integrity of the profession through the practice of the professional. This is achieved through the enforcement of their code of ethics, which may strip their license to practice.

The right to revoke an educator's credential, or license to teach, is not vested in their professional organizations and instead reside in the state boards of education. However, an educator's code of ethics, whether it is developed by a professional organization or by a state may be used to inform the decision as to whether an educator has violated the dismissal or credential revocation standards. Put another way, it may be helpful to borrow from the code of ethics when assessing the conduct and performance of a teacher in the context of a dismissal.

Examples of state adopted codes of ethics include the New Hampshire Department of Education adopted Ed 510: Code of Conduct for New Hampshire Educators in November of 2018. The Code (Ed 510.01) states in "Principle 1—Responsibility to the Education Profession and Educational Professions (a) In fulfilling responsibilities to the education profession and educational professionals, a credential holder shall exemplify honesty and integrity in the course of professional practice."[7]

The Nebraska Department of Education's Standards of Conduct and Ethics for Holders of Public School Certificates lists five principles, which may form the basis for discipline, including admonishment, reprimand, suspension, and revocation.[8] The five principles are as follows:

- Principle I: "The educator shall exhibit good moral character, maintain high standards of performance and promote equality of opportunity in fulfillment of the educator's contractual and professional responsibilities."
- Principle II: "The educator shall work to stimulate the spirit of inquiry, the acquisition of knowledge and understanding, and the thoughtful formulation of worthy goals."
- Principle III: "The educator bears particular responsibility for instilling an understanding of and confidence in the rule of law, a respect for individual freedom, and a responsibility to promote respect by the public for the integrity of the profession."
- Principle IV: "The educator shall believe that sound professional relationships with colleagues are built upon personal integrity, dignity, and mutual respect."
- Principle V: "The Educator shall regard the employment agreement as a pledge to be executed both in spirit and in fact. The educator shall believe that sound personnel relationships with governing boards are built upon personal integrity, dignity, and mutual respect."[9]

THE TEACHER AS A PROFESSIONAL

Historically, school boards have established regulations mandating a higher standard of conduct for teachers than for other community members. Parents who smoked, drank, gambled, lied, and committed adultery demanded that a teacher's conduct be above their own. Traditionally, teachers have been held to a stricter code of conduct precisely because of the role that they have accepted as teachers. "It was and still is believed that teachers must lead an exemplary life so as to properly mold children's virtues."[10] The community decided who should teach its children not just through the teacher selection process but also through the retention process.

It is important to note that their behavior outside of class (as well as inside) continues to be held to a higher standard and can play a part in a decision to dismiss or discipline a teacher. To some teachers, this may seem unfair. However, teachers occupy an important role not just in our schools but also as role models in a community. Teachers occupy a special place in the lives of their students and thus serve as critical guides of an important public good holding a special position of trust and responsibility. The Pennsylvania Supreme Court articulated this role of professional conduct in a 1939 case. The court wrote;

> It has always been the recognized duty of the teacher to conduct himself[/herself] in such a way as to command the respect and goodwill of the community,

though one result of the choice of a teacher's vocation may be to deprive him of the same freedom of action enjoyed by persons in other vocations.[11]

Teachers, as exemplars, are held to a higher standard for the conduct of their private lives than the average citizen because of their relationships to students.

While some of the restrictions on the private lives of teachers have lightened the burden, teachers are still considered to be mandatory role models for their students. This status results in professional obligations that weigh heavily on their actions. The myriad professional responsibilities of the public school teacher frame the discussion on what constitutes causes for dismissal. While the list of causes does not completely fit under this overarching theme of the professional responsibilities of public school teachers, it can be an instructive organization for identifying questionable behaviors.

> The U.S. Supreme Court wrote, "A teacher serves as a role model for [his/her] students, exerting a subtle but important influence over their values and perceptions. Thus, through both the presentation of course materials and the example he sets, a teacher has an opportunity to influence the attitudes of students toward government, the political process, and a citizen's social responsibilities. This influence is crucial to the continued good health of a democracy."
> *Ambach v. Norwick*, 441 U.S. 68, 78–9 (1979).

Noted Stanford professor of research on incompetence in the classroom, Edwin M. Bridges, identified the "I's" of dismissal.[12] Following his early lead on the topic, our review of court cases on teacher dismissal, state statutes defining, and school law secondary sources leads us to confirm Professor Bridges' five causes of action supporting dismissal (illegality, immorality, injury to children, insubordination, and incompetency).

However, they were recast in terms of a breach of professional conduct and retitled "injury to children" to "inappropriate conduct with children." Most often injury to children implicates an illegal act, whereas, some acts may be inappropriate but not illegal, however constituting an unprofessional act. An example is the denigration of a student in front of peers[13] and online.[14] While not illegal, it is clearly inappropriate and a violation of the professional standards of educators.

Below, you will find a brief description of those causes we call the Five Fatal "Eyes" of Unprofessional Conduct. Following Professor Bridges' lead, each cause begins with the letter "I." These categories should not be viewed as silos. Instead they can be overlapping. For example, the sexual abuse of a student is a deep betrayal of professional ethics and is inappropriate conduct with a student, which is illegal and immoral.

Additionally, an act that is illegal can form the basis for dismissal as a separate cause of action. Even allegations of criminal misconduct that have not been decided by a jury or judge can form the basis for a teacher to be terminated. In other words, the higher criminal standard for guilt (e.g., finding that a teacher committed a crime "beyond a reasonable doubt" is not necessarily applicable to a school district's decision to terminate or discipline). For instance, a teacher, during the summer break, fired four shots with one hitting the girlfriend of her estranged husband. She was arrested but was dismissed for immorality before the trial concluded.[15]

But it is the overarching theme of unprofessional conduct that forms the five categories of fatal misconduct. The Fatal "Eyes" are also easier to remember and apply across the states. A short discussion of the Five Fatal "Eyes" follows.

THE FIVE FATAL "EYES" OF THE UNPROFESSIONAL CONDUCT OF EDUCATORS

Inappropriate Conduct with Students

- As a beginning point for the profession, educators must not harm students. Harm is not just physical, such as an injury, a failure to protect a student from foreseeable harm. It also includes sexual abuse, as stated above, and sexual harassment. Conduct that abridges the professional demeanor required of teachers that expects boundaries also constitutes inappropriate conduct.

For example, a teacher used inappropriate physical force on a student by hitting the student on the head with a wooden pointer. This was the fourth incident of such similar behavior.[16] Another teacher purchased and used a cattle prod to discipline students in his sixth grade class.[17] A Tennessee Court of Appeals sustained the dismissal of a teacher finding that the teacher's inappropriate sexual relationship with a student constituted unprofessional conduct.[18]

In California, a second and third grade teacher was dismissed after he became angry and frustrated with his students who were talking and laughing during a classroom movie. He "grabbed some of the students, told them to 'shut up,' 'called them stupid,' struck one student with a chair, hit three students on the top of the head with yardstick or metal desk leg, and threw a pencil or pen at two or three of his students. His conduct frightened the students and in some instances, caused physical pain."[19]

Illegality

- The conviction for certain crimes, especially felonies and crimes against children, may form the basis for dismissal. Examples of dismissal for illegality include the theft of a check from a student, which the court held that the criminal conduct was irremediable.[20] A teacher was "convicted of driving while impaired, had violated the terms of his probation by using drugs and alcohol, had missed 17 days of work as a result of his incarceration, and had provided false reasons for his absence."[21] His dismissal was upheld by the Court of Appeals of Michigan.
- Deilia Butler disclosed on her application in July 2006, for a teaching position with the Fairfax County School Board in Fairfax, Virginia that she had been convicted of a felony drug offense in 1992. In 2012, an investigator informed the school district administration that under existing Virginia law (Coded § 22.1-296.1(A)), a school district cannot hire an individual convicted of a felony. The superintendent recommended Ms. Butler's dismissal based on the fact that the Board had no authority to hire. The Circuit Court held that the Board lacked authority to hire her because of the felony conviction.

The Virginia Supreme Court upheld the Circuit Court's decision. The Board did not have the authority to hire a teacher who had been convicted of a felony, even though the individual taught without disruption. The employment contract was found void "ab intio" (from the beginning).

Immorality

- Charges of immorality have resulted in some of the most tangled and difficult cases. They often sweep in such other causes as inappropriate conduct with students and illegality as well as state statutes identifying immorality as a cause for dismissal as being vague raising a substantive due process concern. A California Court of Appeals in a teacher dismissal case defined immorality in the following manner:

> The term "immoral" has been defined generally as that which is hostile to the welfare of the general public and contrary to good morals. Immorality has not been confined to sexual matters, but includes conduct inconsistent with rectitude, or indicative of corruption, indecency, depravity, dissoluteness; or as willful, flagrant, or shameless conduct showing moral indifference to the opinions

of respectable members of the community, and an inconsiderate toward good order and the public welfare.[22]

Charges of immorality are also brought for out-of-school behavior under the theory of exemplar in which educators are held to the status of mandatory role models. However, this standard was challenged in the latter half of the twentieth century. The California Supreme Court in *Morrison v. State Board of Education*[23] articulated the standard of nexus. This standard seeks to balance the competing legitimate interest of the teacher to have a private life with the community's strong interest in protecting its children from inappropriate or harmful influences.

The nexus standard requires that the private behavior of a teacher could only result in employment sanctions if the conduct affects the teacher's ability to teach or harms the learning environment. The court offered a number of considerations for determining the impact of a teacher's out-of-school conduct on the school setting. These include the following:

1. Would the conduct adversely affect the students or fellow teachers?
2. the proximity or remoteness in time of the conduct;
3. the age of the students that the teacher works with;
4. the extenuating or aggravating circumstances surrounding the conduct;
5. the praiseworthiness or blameworthiness of the motives resulting in the conduct;
6. the likelihood of recurrence; and
7. the extent to which disciplinary action may inflict a chilling effect on the rights of teachers.[24]

Incompetence

- Nathan Essex, a school law professor, defined incompetence as "inefficiency, a lack of skill, inadequate knowledge of subject manner, inability or unwillingness to teach the curricula, failure to work effectively with colleagues and parents, failure to maintain discipline, mismanagement in the classroom, and attitudinal deficiencies."[25] Most often, incompetence is identified through a series of observations and evaluations in which specific deficiencies are documented, defined, and time for remediation with support services are provided. Rarely does one event or one trait lead to a finding of incompetence. Typically, a pattern of behavior emerges through the supervision of a teacher.

A small study ($n = 100$) of Wyoming principal and superintendent perceptions of the traits of incompetent teachers found they agreed on four of the five top traits of incompetence[26] While some traits traded places, for example the principals' top trait "Weak classroom management skills" was first, it was third for superintendents. Each had one in their top five that the other did not. However, the differences between principal and superintendent responses are not statistically significant for these top five traits.

Traits that one would usually associate with teaching practices were in the bottom half of the eighteen traits. The mean scores for these traits follows: "Inability to express content" (principals, M = 2.99 and superintendents, M = 2.97), "Failure to teach curriculum prescribed" (principals, M = 2.85 and superintendents M = 2.97), and "Lack of subject matter knowledge" (principals, M = 2.41 and superintendents, M = 2.43). We offer no explanations for these low scores of these teaching traits of incompetency.

The chart below reflects the top five traits of teacher incompetence as identified by Wyoming principals and superintendents. The survey used Likert-scale items (1 = very uncommon to 4 = very common).[27]

Table 5.1 Wyoming School Leaders Perceptions of the Traits of Teacher Incompetence

Principals' Perceived Traits of Teacher Incompetence (n = 70)	*Superintendents' Perceived Traits of Teacher Incompetence* (n = 30)
1. Weak classroom management skills M = 3.81, SD = 0.43	1. Poor professional judgment M = 3.57, SD 0.078
2. Lack of lesson planning M= 3.43, SD = .076	2. Weak communication with parents M = 3.55, SD 0.74
3. Weak communication with parents M = 3.36, SD = 0.68	3. Weak classroom management skills M = 3.53, SD 0.78
4. Poor professional judgment M = 3.29, SD = 0.82	4. Resistance to school or district initiatives M = 3.48, SD 0.74
5. Low levels of student achievement M = 3.23, SD 0.75	5. Lack of lesson planning M = 3.31, SD = 0.66

Insubordination

- Insubordination is a willful disregard for or a refusal to follow school regulations or legitimate, reasonable official directives.[28] A warning is given to the employee about following the directive or policy.[29] If the employee fails or refuses to follow the directive, a charge of insubordination may follow. For example, a New York teacher's dismissal was upheld when he had been previously warned three times about the inappropriateness of his behavior. The Supreme Court, Appellate Division of New York did "not shock the conscience" upholding his dismissal. The court held,

> Petitioner continued in a pattern of conduct that was clearly irresponsible and inappropriate within the classroom setting. Discussing his own ejaculations,

admonishing a student about putting her legs in the air, telling another student that he should take a good look at a diagram of a woman's vagina because he will not see one otherwise, talking about the color of a student's underwear, and responding to a student's inappropriate comment by remarking about seeing her name on bathroom walls, constitute more than isolated, aberrant behavior. Rather, such conduct is indicative of a continued pattern of offensive behavior that reflect an inability to understand the necessary separation between a teacher and his students.[30]

The Five Fatal "Eyes" is not an exhaustive list or documentation of all the possible scenarios that could lead to dismissal. They do present a framework that encompasses most causes of action,[31] and we suggest that incidents administrators may encounter would likely fall within one, if not more, of these five categories. Most of the court cases chosen resulted in the dismissal being upheld, which happens in the majority of cases.

However, there are also examples of where the school officials did not exercise due diligence, or made assumptions. Courts typically defer to the professional judgment of school administrators regarding dismissal or discipline, but that judgment needs support in fact through effective documentation.

NOTES

1. See Author, *Teacher Tenure – Reasons for Dismissal: 50 State Comparison* (Denver, CO: Education Commission of the States May 2014). Site visited on June 1, 2019, available at http://ecs.force.com/mbdata/mbquestRTL?rep=TT05.

2. Author, *Professional Ethics*, Center for the Study of Ethics in the Professions (Chicago, IL: Illinois Institute of Technology 2008) http://ethics.iit.edu/teaching/professional-ethics.

3. Linda Darling-Hammond, "Accountability for Professional Practice." *Teachers College Record* 91 (1989): 59–80, 67. She further writes, "Professionals are obligated to do whatever is best for the client, not what is easiest, most expedient, or what the client himself or herself might want." Darling-Hammond, "Accountability for Professional Practice."

4. Regina Umpstead, Kevin Brady, Elizabeth Lugg, Joann Klinker, and David Thompson, "Educator Ethics: A Comparison of Teacher Professional Responsibility Laws in Four States." *Journal of Law & Education* 42 (2013): 183–225, 186. Furthermore, they write, "Professional codes of ethics in education concern how educators *ought* to conduct themselves within the profession of education." Umpstead, et al., "Educator Ethics," 188 (emphasis in original).

5. Author, *Model Rules of Professional Conduct: Rule 8.4: Misconduct, Maintaining the Integrity of the Profession* (Chicago, IL: American Bar Association n.d.) https://www.americanbar.org/about_the_aba/contact/.

6. Author, AMA Code of Ethics, *American Medical Association* (June 2001) (e.g., "Principles of Medical Ethics, I. A physician shall be dedicated to providing

competent medical care, with compassion and respect for human dignity and rights."). Site visited on June 1, 2019, available at https://www.ama-assn.org/sites/ama-assn.org/files/corp/media-browser/principles-of-medical-ethics.pdf.

7. Author, Ed 510: Code of Conduct for New Hampshire Educators, *New Hampshire Department of Education* (November 8, 2018). Site visited on December 15, 2018, available at https://www.education.nh.gov/certification/documents/code_conduct.pdf.

8.
- "Admonishment shall mean a private sanction to an educator that further unprofessional or unethical conduct may result in more serious action including suspension or revocation of a certificate."
- "Reprimand shall mean a public sanction criticizing or rebuking an educator for unprofessional or unethical conduct."
- Suspension shall mean a public sanction withdrawing an educator's certificate for a certain period of time. The certificate is automatically reinstated at the expiration of the suspension if it has not expired during the period of suspension."
- "Revocation shall mean a public sanction canceling an educator's certificate for a certain period of time. At the expiration of the revocation period, the former educator may apply for reinstatement."

Nebraska Department of Education, *Standards of Conduct and Ethics for Holders of Public School Certificates* (n.d.). Site visited on June 15, 2019, available at http://nde.ne.gov/CC/standcond.pdf.

9. Ibid.

10. Todd A. DeMitchell and Richard Fossey, *The Limits of Law-Based School Reform: Vain Hopes and False Promises* (Lanham, MD: Technomic Press 1997), 53. ("Traditionally, educators have been compelled to adhere more strictly to the community's moral codes than most other professions or occupations. Teachers have been considered holders of a special position of trust and responsibility because of their relationship with the community's children."). DeMitchell & Fossey, *The Limits of Law-Based School Reform.*

11. *Horosko v. School District of Mount Pleasant Township*, 6 A. 2d 866, 868 (1939).

12. Edwin M. Bridges, *The Incompetent Teacher: Managerial Responses* (Philadelphia: The Falmer Press, 1992).

13. See Representative Assembly, *Code of Ethics* (Washington, DC: National Education Association 1975) "Principle I Commitment to the Student (5) Shall not intentionally expose the student to embarrassment or disparagement." Site visited on February 24, 2019, available at http://www.nea.org/home/30442.htm.

14. Natalie Munroe included in her eighty-four blogs the following descriptions of her students, "rat-like," "dunderhead," "whiny," "frightfully dim," and "jerk." (*Munroe v. Central Bucks School District*, 34 F. Supp. 3d 532, 534 (E.D. Pa. 2014)) All parties agreed that she wrote her blogs as a private citizen, free speech was not abridged. The court concluded, "In this case, [Munroe's] speech, in both effect and tone, was sufficiently disruptive so as to diminish any legitimate interest in its expression, and thus her expression was not protected." Ibid., 541.

15. *Thomas v. Board of Education of Cape Girardeau School District No. 63*, 926 S.W. 2d 163, 165 (Mo. Ct. App. 1996). The Court of Appeals wrote, "We agree with the Board that the intentional shooting of another without legal justification or excuse was sufficiently contrary to justice and good morals to meet the definition of immoral conduct."

16. *Board of Education of West Yuma School District RJ-1 v. Flaming*, 938 P.2d 151 (Colo. 1997).

17. *Rolando v. School Directors of District No. 125*, 358 N.E.2d 945 (Ill. App. Ct. 1976). The court, concluding that the teacher's behavior was irremediable, wrote, "We conclude that there is no place in the public school system of our State for the use of cattle prods as a means of enforcing discipline." Ibid., 949.

18. *Crosby v. Holt*, 320 S.W. 3d 805 (Tenn. Ct. App. 2009).

19. *DeYoung v. Commission on Professional Competence*, 228 Cal. App. 4th 568, 572 (2014).

20. *McBroom v. Board of Education, District No. 205*, 494, N.E. 2d 1191, 1198 (App. Crt. 2 Dist. 1986) (writing, "Teachers, as leaders and role models, with their education and background, have the duty to implant basic societal values and qualities of good citizenship in their students. To claim that such conduct was remediable distorts the thrust and purpose of the rule. Criminal activity of this nature is conduct which cannot be remedied by a warning.").

21. *Cona v. Avondale School District*, 842 N.W. 2d 277, 289 (2013).

22. *San Diego Unified School District v. Commission on Professional Competence*, 124 Cal. Rptr. 3d 320, 329 (App. 4 Dist. 2011).

23. *Morrison v. State Board of Education* 461 P.2d 375 (Cal. 1969).

24. Ibid., 386. For a discussion of the theory of nexus, *see* Todd A. DeMitchell, Suzanne Eckes, and Richard Fossey, "Sexual Orientation and the Public School Teacher." *Boston University Public Interest Law Journal* 19 (2009): 65–105, 74–79.

25. Nathan Essex, *School Law and the Public Schools: A Practical Guide for Educational Leaders* (5th Ed.) (Upper Saddle River, NJ: Pearson Education 2012), 255.

26. Bret G. Range, Heather E. Duncan, Susan Day Scherz, & Courtney A. Haines. (2012). "School Leaders' Perceptions About Incompetent Teachers: Implications for Supervision and Evaluation" *NASSP Bulletin* 96(4): 302-22.

27. Ibid., 311.

28. The Supreme Court of Indiana in *McKay v. State ex rel. Young*, 212 Ind. 338, 340 (1937) found that the dismissal of a teacher for insubordination and incompetency was not sustained by the evidence. The teacher signed her contract with her maiden name having married a year earlier. She did not disclose her marital status. The dismissal letter stated referring to her status, "The Board feels that they are entitled to know the marital status of their teachers, as such status may have a direct bearing upon the nature of the work and assignment given to her the following year." The court held that there was no legal requirement for teachers to disclose their marital status. Consequently, there was no legal basis for the dismissal. Insubordination is predicated upon the employer issuing a legal directive.

29. See Section VI below A. Notes to File: From the Informal Communication to Formal Documentation for an example of documenting a case of insubordination that also turned into unprofessional conduct.

30. *Lackow v. Department of Education of the City of New York*, 51 A.D. 3d 563, 569 (N.Y.A.D. 1 Dept. 2008).

31. For example, school law scholars Martha McCarthy, Nelda H. Cambron-McCabe, and Suzanne Eckes, *Public School Law: Teachers' and Students' Rights* (Boston: Pearson) conclude, "The most frequently cited statutory causes are incompetency, immorality, insubordination, and neglect of duty" 367. Neglect of duty is cited as a statutory cause for dismissal in a number of states and is often described as a "failure to carry assigned duties" 373.

Chapter 6

Files, Memos, and Documentation

> "The primary objective of a school district's employee evaluation system is to improve employees' performance so they can become successful and contribute to achieving the district's goals. . . . The district's evaluation system thus serves as secondary function—the removal of the unsatisfactory employee."[1]

The evaluation, remediation, and possible dismissal of a teacher requires a quality documentation system that substantiates the concluding employment decision. "Memories inevitably fade over time, but documentation is the best way to preserve a record of the steps you have taken and the reasons for your actions, decisions, preparing you to defend them should the need arise."[2] Memorializing information in the written word, or through an organized system, mitigates this issue. Moreover, documentation created "contemporaneous" to any incident has evidentiary value, if an adverse employment decision is challenged.

The records that we keep affect people in powerful ways. Documents written regarding employee performance are statements that stand-alone and speak independent of the principal/administrator. They should be written for three parties: the adversarial, the supportive, and the independent. A disciplinary memo must

- be clear, concise, and truthful;
- be specific and relevant to the teacher and the issue at hand;
- be objective, reporting all the relevant facts, including prior assistance that has been offered as well;
- contain specific recommendations for improvement since the supervision/evaluation process is aimed at developing, maintaining, and improving teaching skills and behaviors[3];

- provide a clear warning that future disciplinary action that might be taken for a failure to heed the directive(s);
- provide a statement of the employee's right to attach a response to the memorandum that is placed in their personnel file; and
- must not contain any sarcasm, innuendo, or statements that signify a personal conflict or animus.

DOCUMENTATION

Not all documentation is the same. It involves several types of written memoranda used for several purposes.[4] We provide examples for three types of documents. The first is Notes to File: From Informal Communication to Formal Documentation. The second is a Single Incident Memorandum. The third is a Remediation Memorandum.

A. Notes to File: From Informal Communication to Formal Documentation

Not every communication with an employee rises to the level of formal documentation placed in the employees personnel file. Often principals will write a short memo on an issue (e.g., teacher was late to duty) and the principal wishes to note and remind the employee about the behavior. This memo most likely will not be placed in the personnel file as a documented formal memorandum.

Principals often keep memo communication files that are meant to provide a history of events, commitments, and reminders. These files are organizational tools and memory aids and not official personnel files and are often referred to as "desk drawer notes," meaning that they are meant to be kept in the drawer/possession of the writer. These are not shared with others.

The principal may either communicate with the teacher via a short email in which the memo would go into the communication file and/or the principal may want to just handle it more informally as a discussion but wants to remember it and places it in notes to file.

The last type of file is the official personnel file. This file has a custodian of-the-record who is tasked with maintaining and securing the file. The personnel file may contain basic information on the employee including personal information, compensation, employment-related agreements, as well as evaluation-related documents. Employees have access to this file under certain guidelines designed to give access and to protect the documents. Disciplinary memos and remediation plans are placed in this file with proper notice to the employee.

Only documents/memos that the employee has seen and has had the opportunity to respond verbally and in writing can be used in a disciplinary proceeding. Employees have the right to append their response to document/memos in their personnel file and this response, too, will become part of the file. General communication memos and notes to file cannot be used to support discipline unless they are incorporated into a memorandum that is discussed with the employee and it is clearly stated that the memo is being placed in the personnel file.

A hypothetical example, noted below, illustrates the interaction of these ideas and parts of documentation, including the following: Notes to the File, A General Communication File (of correspondence sent), Personnel File Documentation. We are going to follow a teacher who has occasionally been late or missed his duty assignments. The principal is concerned that a pattern is starting to develop and starts with notes to file and progresses to documentation placed in the teacher's personnel file.

1. The Background

Noah Dutee, a middle-school math teacher, has trouble showing up for his assigned bus duty. He does not see standing duty as part of his professional responsibilities and often voices his opinion that it is low-level responsibility and that his skills and expertise are better used in different activities. He holds the position that his preparation never included the requirement that he stand bus duty, or any duty. His protestations have increased lately gaining the attention of the faculty and the principal, Dr. B. A. Pepper. Pepper's "Notes to the File" is below.

2. Principal's Notes to File

September 9, 20XX: Noah did not show up for his assigned bus duty.
September 23, 20XX: Noah did not show up for his assigned bus duty.
September 27, 20XX Noah was at least 10 minutes late for bus duty.
October 7, 20XX: Noah was not on bus duty. I looked for him and found him in the teachers' lounge. I reminded him that he was late for duty.
October 11, 20XX: Noah was not on bus duty when I went out to check. I covered his duty. Talked with him afterwards, asking why he was not on duty and reminded him that he needed to be on duty on time. A pattern appears to be emerging, need to step up observations. He wouldn't have another duty for two weeks
October 21, 20XX: Noah was not on duty. I found him and told him that he had duty and that he needed to report to duty. He gave me an excuse that he forgot and left for his duty.
October 24, 20XX: Noah was not at his duty station. I talked to him at the end of the day. He said that he objects to it as unprofessional and a waste

of his talents. I told him that it was his professional responsibility to show up for duty and that we would meet the next morning during his planning period to discuss the issue and my concerns. I had a parent conference that I had to attend. I am concerned.

3. Principal's General Communication File

This memo is still a general communication memo and has not been placed into the official personnel file. It is not a disciplinary memo, because no discipline has been instituted. It is a memo restating responsibilities. It is also a general type memo that often is written following a meeting to ensure that there is an understanding of what occurred.

The problem continues and Noah has missed his duty assignment on November 9. Dr. Pepper contacted Noah the following day about a meeting via the following email communication.

> *"Noah, I have set a meeting for us to discuss my concerns about your continued failure to stand your bus duty, including missing your duty to this morning as part of your professional responsibilities. The meeting time and place is stated below. Your first period class will be covered. Because discipline may result from this meeting you may bring a union representative to the meeting.[5] Assistant Principal Ima H. Alper will attend."*

4. Documentation Placed in the Personnel File

TO: Noah Dutee
FR: B.A. Pepper, Ph.D.
DT: November 11, 20XX
RE: Summary of Conference (11.11.XXXX) Regarding Unprofessional Conduct and Insubordination

This memorandum is a summary of the conference held this morning in my office. In addition to the two of us, you invited a union representative, Les W. Ork and I asked assistant principal Ima H. Alper to attend.

The purpose of the meeting was to discuss my concern about your failure to consistently meet your professional responsibility to be on time and to attend to your duty assignments.

At our meeting of October 26th I discussed my concern with you about your failure to report to your duty station on 10/7/XXXX, 10/11/XXXX, 10/21/XXXX, and 10/25/XXXX (see Appendix A). I stated that your professional responsibilities include meeting your duty obligations.

On November 9th you once again failed to show up for duty and I set up this meeting (see Appendix B). At the meeting I recounted the five times you have missed your duty assignment in about a month. You offered no explanation as to why you have missed such a significant number of duties other than you don't believe that you should have to stand a duty. This is an insufficient response to your failure to meet your professional obligations.

I am very concerned about your behavior of not showing up for duty. The duties are shared responsibilities for the faculty. They are important assignments in that they help to provide a safe environment for our students by providing proper supervision. Failure to provide supervision increases the potential for harm and injury to students.

Mr. Ork asked whether all faculty are assigned duties and whether any of them also have been called into disciplinary meetings. I responded that all faculty members have additional duty assignments. I also stated that I cannot discuss specific employee matters in this meeting, and that I have discussed privately with a teacher if he/she appears to be establishing a pattern of not meeting professional expectations, which is what I did with you before we had our first meeting to discuss my concerns about your behavior.

Your intentional acts of not showing up for five duty assignments in a short period of time is evidence of unprofessional conduct in that you failed to meet your clearly stated professional responsibility in a consistent manner (See Appendix C faculty Handbook and reminders to staff about duty assignments). Furthermore, your failure to report to duty on November 9th is an act of insubordination. The meeting and follow up memorandum of November 9th clearly stated the expectation that you attend to your duty assignment in a professional and timely manner. Within a short period of time you intentionally disregarded this directive to attend to your duty assignment. This is an act of insubordination.

You are hereby directed to consistently and timely attend to your duty assignments. Failure to heed this directive may result in further disciplinary action up to and including dismissal or non-renewal of your contract. Please refer to RSA 189:13 and RSA 189:14-a as authority in this serious matter (see Appendix D).

A copy of this memorandum and appendices will be placed in your personnel file in ten days. You have the right to attach comments to this memorandum.

―――――――――――――――――――――――――――――   ――――――――
B. A. Pepper, Ph.D., Principal   Date
I have received a copy of this Memorandum with appendices. My signature does not necessarily mean that I agree with its contents.

―――――――――――――――――――――――――――――   ――――――――
Noah Dutee.   Date
Cc: Personnel File
         Les W. Ork, Union Representative
         Ima H. Alper, Assistant Principal

This memo is given to Noah personally. Give him the opportunity to review the document and ask questions. Consider having your assistant principal attend that short meeting. If Noah refuses to sign the memo, don't force the situation, just ask your assistant to sign with date and time and a short statement that a copy of the memo was given to Noah. Send copies of the memo to the two attendees of the meeting.

SINGLE INCIDENT MEMORANDUM

This documentation differs from the example above in that it involves a single incident as opposed to an evolving situation. It essentially is a snapshot focusing on an incident with a specific time frame. This type of a memorandum may arise from a complaint or from a third party. Frels et al. recommends in these situations a written complaint should be solicited and used as a basis for an investigation of the facts.[6] This should be followed by a conference with the teacher if the facts support taking this step.

Sometimes, the facts arise out of a situation in which the principal is an observer or a participant. The following example of a single incident memorandum is one in which the principal is a participant.[7]

LAKESIDE MIDDLE SCHOOL

TO: Mina Fafree
FR: Donna Mess-Witme, Principal
DT: December 6, 20XX
RE: Disciplinary Memorandum

This memorandum is a summary of our meeting on December 5th regarding the following incident. Your invited union representative was present as was the school assistant's principal. These two individuals listened but did not participate in the meeting.

On December 4, 20XX the school received a delivery from Classroom Friendly Books. The delivery included a DVD player and a confirming fax of the full order you placed for two 27-inch television sets, a microwave oven, and the DVD player which were delivered. Upon receiving the delivery and the confirmation order for more merchandise, I became concerned about the propriety of the purchases. Having two 27-inch televisions in our classrooms is highly unusual, and we do not use microwaves in our sixth grade classrooms as per our policy. Consequently, I contacted the Assistant Superintendent, Dr. Guy Moovinup. He asked me to check on how these purchases were going to be used in the instructional program. He stated that teachers could not use funds that were generated through an employee's work especially when school and student funds are used. I brought the DVD player to your room but waited outside because you had a student in your classroom and there was a parent in a classroom next to yours. The following exchange took place between the two of us, which was overheard in significant part by Mr. Stan D. Round.

- *After bringing the cart with DVD player to the hallway outside your classroom, I asked you about the instructional purposes for the purchases. You responded that they were for your personal use. You had purchased them using your personal bonus points.*
- *I asked you to cancel the order and return the merchandise because it was purchased through the funds provided by individual students, other teachers, and through school funds in addition to the books that you bought for your personal use.*
- *You refused stating that the points were yours and that you could use then in any manner that you chose and that you would take them home for your personal use. You stated that no one ever told you that you could not use the book bonus points in this manner.*
- *By this time Mr. Round had walked into the hallway with you on his right and me on his left. Through his written statement, he stated that he heard me say, "It's illegal. It isn't your money to spend."*
- *I further stated that I had checked with Assistant Superintendent Moovinup and he confirmed that it was inappropriate for you to use the bonus points gained through your employment for your personal use.*
- *You responded, "He is full of crap. I'm not packing up anything up and sending it anywhere with one arm." You had stated that you had injured your arm.*
- *As you turned to leave you said so that Mr. Round heard it as well, "This school sucks." You concluded with the statement, "Forget it, and keep the stuff."*

As I stated in the meeting your behavior, described above, is unprofessional. You used your position as a teacher for personal gain. The bonus points were not solely generated by the use of your personal funds. Students bought books, your colleagues bought books, and the school bought books through your account. The materials that you bought using the funds of others were not yours to use as you wish.

You violated Section 3.14 of the Personnel Policy Manual, as well as the National Education Association's Code of Ethics, which prohibits a teacher using her/his professional relationship with students for private advantage (Principle I, #7). Your use of student funds to purchase books which you in turn used the generated bonus points for your private advantage is unprofessional.

Furthermore, your use of bonus points for purchases made by the school for your private use violates Section 6.02 of the Personnel Policy Manual. When given the opportunity to find a solution in which the materials would be used by the school or would be returned without violating the authorities cited above, you chose to say that you would use the points in any manner that you choose. It wasn't until you left the discussion with an off-hand comment to forget it and to keep the stuff that you relented. However, the nature of your remark did not communicate an understanding of your professional commitments to your students and to the school.

In addition, you were unprofessional when you told me, in front of another teacher and in the hallway with at least one student in the vicinity that "This school sucks." This conduct was made without regard for the presence of others who were in the vicinity; it denigrates the school and its employees; and uses language that does not reach the expected level of discussion between professional educators even when, and especially when, they may disagree.

Your unprofessional behavior must cease. You are directed to not use Classroom Friendly Book Bonus Points for your personal use when they are generated by the purchases of others including students, teachers, and the school. You are further directed to not engage in unprofessional conduct such as stating within the hearing of students, parents, faculty, and staff that "this school sucks." You have the first amendment right, which I will protect, to express professional disagreements with the policies, and practices. But those statements must be professional in nature using language that is acceptable as a professional educator and in an appropriate place.

Failure to follow the directives contained in this memorandum will result in further disciplinary action up to any including dismissal or non-renewal of your contract. Please refer to RSA 189:13 and RSA 189:14-a as authority in this serious matter.

This official letter of reprimand will be placed in your personnel file. You have ten days in which you may append comments to this memorandum.

Donna Mess-Witme, Principal   *Date*
I have received a copy of this memorandum. My signature does not necessarily constitute agreement with its contents.

Mina Fafree   *Date*
Cc: *Personnel File*
       Union Representative
       Assistant Principal
       Guy Moovinup, Ed.D., Assistant Superintendent
Attachments:
       Personnel Policy Manual, Section 3.14
       Personnel Policy Manual, Section 6.02

National Education Association, Code of Ethics
RSA 189:13
RSA 189:14-a

REMEDIATION MEMORANDUM

A remediation memorandum creates a larger picture of the work of an employee over time than a single incident memorandum. It includes several incidents or a series of observations and evaluations. It is a signal that specific behaviors are unacceptable and must be addressed and remediated.[8] However, generally it is not considered an adverse employment action, instead its purpose is to "identify and correct deficiencies in a teacher's teaching method."[9]

An interesting alternative to the remediation memorandum is a "Last Chance Agreement" (LCA). This type of agreement is usually used when the suspect behavior is irremediable and thus a remediation plan would be inappropriate—the behavior must not occur again. The signed LCA means that the teacher "waives his[/her] right to contest termination in the case of a future violation."[10]

Providing a clear and reasonable remediation/professional development plan identifying weakness that must be overcome through assistance and strategies is critical. For example, a New York teacher contested his unsatisfactory rating in the New York state courts. The principals and two assistant principals through their observations found poor performance in classroom management, lesson planning, and student engagement.[11]

A plan was developed for the teacher. The Supreme Court of New York held that the rating had a rational basis. Furthermore, the court found that the plan identified areas of improvement and made "specific recommendations for addressing continuing deficiencies."[12] The plan should not just focus on getting a "passing grade" on the remediation plan, but, instead, the educator must focus on changing his or her teaching behaviors on a daily basis.

The remediation plan must be shaped by and conform to state law on teacher dismissal, any procedural or substantive requirements in the collective bargaining agreement, applicable school district documents (e.g., board policy, evaluation plans), and national and/or state codes of ethics. The following are some potential guidelines for writing a remediation document. A selection of examples, in italics, adapted from an actual remediation plan follows each point.

1. Clearly identify the concern(s) with the teacher's performance using data that had been previously available to and discussed with the employee.

This notice of incompetency is based on sixteen (16) observations and memos all of which were previously discussed with you. The specific findings of incompetency based on state law (§ 44937) district expectations and performance indicators are as follows:

Establishment and Maintenance of a Suitable Learning Environment
Lack of Classroom Control

- *The following ten (10) communications (see Exhibit A) evidence a lack of student control in your in your classroom: [list the dates of the memos]*
- *A sample of the observations of this deficiency include [more samples are provided in the memorandum]:*

> *"Thirty-one outbursts occurred during the time you read the vocabulary definitions and fill-in from the handout." (9/16/20XX)*

> *"A student set fire to a piece of paper during your fourth period class and threw it across the room. You did nothing." (10/28/20XX)*

Instructional Techniques and Strategies

- *Lack of High Learning Time*
- *Failure to Use a Variety of Teaching Strategies Designed to Stimulate and Engage Students*
- *It has been noted in eight (8) communications (See Exhibit B) that your teaching strategies have not fostered high academic learning time. In addition, you have failed to consistently use a variety of techniques and strategies designed to engage students as active participants in a stimulating activity that challenges while providing for a high rate of success.*
- *A sample of observations of these deficiencies include [more samples are provided in the memorandum]:*

> *"Students read orally from the textbook, interrupted by copying verbatim from the text. There were no questioning strategies employed nor any teaching strategies that would enable the students to become actively engaged with the material." (12/2/20XX)*

> *"Of the 14 questions asked, none were a high cognitive level." (1/14/20XX)*

2. State the consequences of a failure to overcome the deficiencies.

I am advising you of deficiencies in your performance that fall within the meaning of "incompetency" as that term is used in Education Code section 44938. This code section provides that at least 90 days before a governing board may take action to terminate employment of a certified employee because of incompetence, a notice must be sent to the employee informing him/her of the nature of his/her incompetence and identifying specific instances with the goal of affording the employee the opportunity to improve his/her job performance.

Failure to satisfactorily meet the standards stated in the document will result in a recommendation to the school board that they dismiss you from employment in the school district.

3. Set a reasonable timeline for completion of the plan.

As stated above, the employee has 90 days from the receipt of the memorandum to complete the plan before a decision is made regarding the disposition of the plan—plan successfully completed, a continuation of the plan, or dismissal will be recommended to the Board of Education.

4. Establish Progress Points to Review Progress

Because these meetings are part of the potential disciplinary proceeding, you may invite a union representative to the meetings. A memo summarizing the findings and conclusions of the meeting will be developed and shared with the participants.

You will be observed a minimum of six (6) times during the next 90 days. You will participate in a review conference near the 30, 60, and 90 day marks to assess your progress. Because these review conferences may result in disciplinary action you may bring a union representative to these meetings. The Director of Personnel & Labor Relations will generate a summary memorandum following each review meeting and distribute it to the participants.

SAMPLE NINETY-DAY INCOMPETENCY PROGRESS MEETING MEMORANDUM

TO: <Teacher>
FR: <Administrator in charge of the meeting>
DT: XX/XX/XXXX
RE: Second Progress Meeting of the 90-Day Notice of Incompetency

On XX/XX/XXXX at 10:04AM we met, with the principal and your representative in attendance, to discuss your progress toward competency. This is the second meeting of your 90-day Notice of Incompetency. As per the Notice, we will hold one more progress meeting before a recommendation is made whether you have successfully met the standards for competency.

I discussed the documents developed since the last meeting including formal observations, student disciplinary referrals, and communications with parents, as well as the log of remedial activities that you took part in. All documents are appended to this memorandum. In addition, I reviewed my notes of my twenty minute unannounced visit two days prior to this meeting.

At the conclusion of the review, I stated that you are still deficient and incompetent in the two areas identified in your Notice of Incompetency.

Your representative, XX, asked what help had been given to you in overcoming your deficiencies. I discussed the use of the mentor and other personnel who were tasked with assisting XX. At one point in the discussion you indicated that the help was not as productive as you hoped, stating that XX, your mentor teacher considered you "a lost cause." I reminded you that you have been working with mentors and others since last year. In addition, the administration has offered specific recommendations to be implemented by you to help overcome your deficiencies.

I asked what additional assistance you would like to have from the administration. You responded with two requests and one statement.

Your first request was to observe other classrooms. I responded that I would set up two out of district observations (see copy of follow-up memos requesting visitations at two neighboring school districts). The principal stated that she would set up observations of other classes within the school. Substitute teachers would be provided as needed.

Your second request was where to start your instruction for the second semester XX class. The principal stated that you could start with any unit that you chose. However, she highly recommended that you select the unit that makes pedagogical sense and that it reflect what you consider to be your greatest strength so that you can be successful from the start.

In response to my query if you had other requests or statements, you replied yes that you had a statement. You stated that there was a lack of administrative support. When asked to expand you said that you have to contact parents more than other teachers. The principal replied that your statement was true. However, contacting parents is part of the school's discipline plan and since you have a large number of disciplinary referrals, you would according to the disciplinary policy have to contact a large number of parents. You agreed with me that contacting parents is an obligation and duty of teachers. I stated that the support that you have received in handling referrals was appropriate. I cited, as an example, how I witnessed during my recent twenty-minute informal drop-in observation that I observed a student in your class set fire to a piece of paper that he had spayed with hair spray and threw it across the room. Before I could get out of my seat to check on the flaming paper it immediately extinguished upon hitting the floor. The assistant principal upon my notice to him intervened removing and disciplining the student. I noted that you took no action.

The meeting was adjourned at 11:06AM

Cc: Principal, XX
      Representative, XX

5. **State Professional Development Activities that Can be Accessed, Including Resources and Personnel**

Remediation Plan

The principal, assistant principal, and the assistant superintendent for instruction have given you specific remedial strategies in overcoming your deficiencies. In addition to these strategies, you have been given the opportunity and encouragement to attend workshops, observe teachers, and work with mentor teachers.

You are directed to do the following in order to demonstrate competence in the above stated areas:

1. *consistently demonstrate through observations that you are employing effective classroom management techniques that create a business-like atmosphere conducive to student learning;*
2. *consistently demonstrate through observations, review of lesson plans, and class assignments that you are actively engaging your students in the lesson; and*
3. *effectively and consistently use more appropriate teaching strategies.*

In addition to the observations and review conferences, you are directed to participate in the following activities:

A. *continue to work with mentor teachers;*
B. *go on at least two (2) classroom visits to other school that the administration will set up;*
C. *read and implement the strategies outlined in Brophy et al. as well as other instructional authors that will be provided for you;*
D. *review and implement strategies from provided materials on such topics as alternative teaching strategies, such as higher cognitive questioning techniques, inquiry methods of instruction, Madeline Hunter's lesson design, etc.*
E. *implement previously discussed strategies for classroom control found in the attached exhibits;*
F. *review materials in exhibits and previously provided on establishing quality relations with parents; and*
G. *develop and communicate high expectations for all students in all of your classes.*

6. **Hold a conference at the conclusion of the remediation plan timeline and issue a memorandum either leading to a dismissal proceeding, the**

conclusion of the remediation of the plan with concerns sufficiently remediated, or the development of a new remediation plan.

The consistent use of an effective system of documentation is neither fast nor easy. It is hard work that requires a high level of expertise and a commitment to quality teaching. Luckily, the great majority of teachers are hardworking, dedicated professionals who are effective. But what about the minority of teachers, the ones that Judge Treu in the California tenure case *Vergara v. State*, labeled "grossly ineffective"[13] those teachers at the bottom of the bell curve of effectiveness? Are they adequately supervised and remediated, or if improvement is not achieved are they induced to exit the profession? Or are they and more importantly their students allowed to languish in the classroom, marking time to the ring of the next bell?

Principals and superintendents who make quality education come alive as a theory in use and not just an espoused theory by insisting on the rendering of professional services by all who are employed to work with students, probably help to improve their schools by a larger measure than any spate of reform reports that are generated outside the schoolhouse gate. The most lasting reform is the professional commitment made by educators daily to students, fellow educators, and the community to render quality service.

NOTES

1. Kelly Frels, Janet L. Horton, Lisa McBride, & Ilya Feldsherov, *A Documentation System for Teacher Improvement or Termination* (7th Ed.) (Cleveland, OH: Education Law Association, 2014), 43.

2. Kimberly M. Bandy, Natalie C. Schaefer, and Roberta F. Green, "Teacher Evaluation: The Legal Factors," Communicator 36 (February 2013), https://www.naesp.org/communicator-february-2013/teacher-evaluation-legal-factors.

3. The dismissal of a tenured teacher was overturned by an Arizona Court of Appeals when the teacher convincingly argued that the "reminder letter" issued by the principal did not constitute notice of inadequacy. The court noted that letter failed to specify the teacher's remediable deficiencies so as to "furnish the teacher an opportunity to correct his inadequacies and overcome the grounds for charge." *Orth v. Phoenix Union High School System*, 613 P.2d 311, 313 (Ariz. Ct. App. 1980).

4. Frels, et al., *supra* note 1, 8.

5. The right to representation is found in *NLRB v. J. Weingarten Co.*, 420 U.S. 251, 262–263 (1975), which held that the union is required to protect employee's rights without interfering with the legitimate prerogatives of the employer. For a discussion of the role (silent observer or advocate) of the union in such meetings, *see* Jodie Meade Michalski, "Knowing When to Keep Quiet: *Weintgarten* and the Limitations on Representative Participation." *Hofstra Labor & Employment Law* 26 (2008): 163–192.

6. Frels, et al., *supra* note 1, 11.

7. This scenario is based on *Timpani v. Lakeside School Dist.*, 386 S.W.3d 588 (Ark. App. 2011). Minor changes were made to allow the fact pattern to fit into the format of a single incident memorandum. In this case, the school district dismissed the teacher. The teacher lost at trial.

8. This type of documentation is sometimes referred to as a "growth plan." See Frels, et al., *supra* note 1, 15.

9. *Moss v. Texarkana Arkansas School District*, 240 F.Supp.3d, 966, 974 (W.D. Ark. 2017) (concluding, "Thus, the improvement plan alone cannot amount to an adverse employment action."). Ibid.

10. *Bain v. Wrend*, 2018 WL 5980376 (November 14, 2018) *2.

11. *Cohen v. Board of Education of City School District*, 960 N.Y.S.2d 362, 363 (A.D. 1 Dept. 2013).

12. Ibid.

13. *Vergra v. State*, No. BC484642, 2014 WL 2598719 at *2 (Cal. Super. Ct. L.A. Cty. June 10, 2014).

Chapter 7

Conclusion and the Ten Commandments of Documentation

"The evaluation of teachers calls for transparent, rigorous, and fair systems."[1]

As stated in Chapter 1, "Who teaches matters"[2] is a simple truth but a complex imperative for action. A 2018 Gallup poll of superintendents found that 84 percent of the respondents stated that recruiting and retaining talented teachers was a major challenge, in fact the number one challenge.[3] Educational leaders have a commitment to provide and sustain conditions in which teacher professionalism can flourish to the benefit of students. Part of this commitment involves staff development, supervision, and evaluation. Our commentary has briefly explored the role of documentation in supervision and evaluation.

While the challenges that educational leaders face in properly supervising, evaluating, and documenting employee performance are real, as Professor Larry E. Frase stated decades ago, administrators must *"keep in mind their primary goal: putting only competent teachers in contact with students."*[4] Concomitantly, the employee's right and desire to receive accurate feedback on her or his professional efforts argues for the employment of an effective, valid, and fairly implemented supervision system. Teachers have just as much of a vested interest in quality schools as administrators and parents. They want to work in a good school with competent colleagues.[5] Their end-of-the-year evaluation should not be a surprise; all employees should have a good idea if their performance meets the standards or is in need of improvement because the evaluator has worked with the employee identifying concerns. The flip side of the coin is that employees who are doing an excellent job need to have their success reinforced and those who are making progress toward excellence also need feedback from a quality evaluation to identify strengths so they can be shored up and their weakness addressed.

The teacher must also make a good faith effort to implement the strategies, approaches, and come to the remediation process with the desire to respond appropriately to the plan. For example, a curriculum director developed a dysfunctional working environment through his unprofessional conduct of refusing to "come out of his office and attend meetings to discuss curriculum" with teachers.[6] The Supreme Court of Nebraska held "that professional conduct required an ability to respond to criticism in a healthy way."[7] Responsibility is a two-way street.

Employees should expect to have ongoing conversations on their instruction and student affairs and to receive reviews based on observations in an environment of mutual respect with a focus on student achievement in a supportive, safe environment. They should expect to receive timely notice of concerns about their professional practice so as to be able to respond to the concerns and make appropriate adjustments.

School administrators should expect that employees will appropraitely engage with the school administrator and respond at a professional level to the concerns, recommendations, and requirements regarding the employee's professional service. Their community of interests—a mutual focus on the best interests of their students—must guide the supervision and evaluation process. Performance evaluation must be accurate and fair, balancing the interests of the school and the individual.

We offer the following Ten Commandments of Documentation as a guide to help steady the hand as the needle of supervision, evaluation, and documentation is threaded.

THE TEN COMMANDMENTS OF DOCUMENTATION

1. Documentation affects people in powerful ways.[8]
   - It is a statement that stands alone and speaks independent of the administrator.
   - "Spoken words are easily forgotten."[9]
2. Documentation is written for three parties.
   - The supportive party—for example, school administrators
   - The adversarial party—for example, the union and other employees
   - The neutral party—This can be a school board, an arbitrator, or a judge—someone who will consider your documentation and render a decision. What does the neutral party need to know?
   - Provide documentation to only those who need to know. Employees have the right to a confidential process.
   - If the document is placed in the personnel file, notice of the placement must be written on the document including time for the educator to append written comments to the document. Please see samples of

documents above in "Documentation Placed in Personnel File" and "Single Incident Memorandum." Provide a place for the employee to sign acknowledging receipt of the document. If the employee chooses not to sign it, do not press the issue, just have our assistant whom you have brought with you sign a copy of the document that it was presented to the employee and date it with the time and whomever may be present.

3. Conference first, write second.[10]
   - Documents are best written in the first person.
   - Conferencing first allows you to gather the facts and a possible explanation for the behavior.
   - Be clear about the issue during the conference, the employee's behavior, and stay on the issue, do not become sidetracked.
4. Establish the facts.
   - It must be accurate, using observed behavior and/or artifacts.
   - The facts must lead to and support the conclusion.
5. Apply the facts.
   - Apply the facts to an expected standard of conduct.
   - "Conclusory statements, inflammatory language, and/or opinions not supported by the facts should be avoided."[11]
6. Documentation must be objective.
   - Use legal authority, such as school policies collective bargaining agreements, board policy, state statutes, and federal statutes when appropriate.[12]
   - Do not draw conclusions that are not supported by the evidence presented in the documentation.
7. Documentation must be complete, but concise and clear.
   - Review past observations, evaluations, and documentation to ascertain if the behavior in question is part of a pattern.
   - Only use documentation that the employee has already had access to and has had a chance to respond to its content.
8. Documentation must provide clear directions and communicate expectations by coming to the point.
   - Directions to the employee must be clear and not vague.[13]
   - A good rule of thumb comes from substantive due process: Would the reasonable person (teacher) know what to do or what not to do upon reading the directions?[14]
   - We must be mindful of our natural tendency to be supportive, often overlooking and or minimizing inappropriate behaviors. (See Toolbox Document D The Bologna Sandwich Technique)
   - What does the employee need to do or not do to improve her/his professional practice to bring it to an acceptable level?
   - Come to a conclusion.

9. Statutory deadlines must be met.
   - If state law requires that notice of a nonrenewal (part of due process) must be received by a specific date, the administration must meet that deadline.
   - Failure to meet the deadline may result in the school board's intended action being voided.
   - This is a failure of an administrator's organizational skills that can have real consequences of retaining an incompetent teacher or the granting of tenure to one who has not earned it.
10. Documentation must be fair.
    - Employees deserve a fair process.
    - A fair process, applying fair laws, communicated and enforced in a fair manner are not only critical, they are due process.
    - Expect fairness from everyone, including yourself.
    - Be firm, but fair.
    - A fair process of judging professional competence is "measured against the standard required of others performing the same or similar duties," it is not measured against a standard of perfection.[15]

Ethical teacher evaluation policies coupled with the ethical application of the policy through the use of these principles should be an important part of the evaluation system and its documentation component. As noted above, teachers are the core of the relationship with students and because of this role they must be treated in an ethical manner. Placing and retaining effective teachers in classrooms and removing ineffective teachers must be grounded in an ethical approach.

Given the importance of education to our nation and to its people,[16] staffing classrooms with highly qualified teachers "is a critical national concern."[17] Jennifer Rice comments, "Teacher quality matters. In fact, it is the most important school-related factor

influencing student achievement."[18] Proper supervision assists with strengthening the instructional skills of the teacher and maintaining a professional classroom is an important responsibility of the principal. Knowledge of how to fairly and properly document performance is important, if not a critical skill for school leaders.

Consistently using a fair process in evaluations and observations assists in supporting the perception by the school faculty that pettiness, vindictiveness, and the vagaries of decision making are not the *modus operandi* of the principal. Consequently, the decision of whom to place and to keep in front of students, how to assist that teacher to reach higher levels of excellence, when to identify deficiencies, and when to dismiss are critical.

The evaluation process cannot just be a ceremonial congratulation, the awarding of a certificate of participation in the school's activities or a certificate of attendance. Who we place and retain in our classrooms is a challenge demanding an imperative of action for school leaders. It must be undertaken with the application of skills and knowledge, and pursued with a high level of professional responsibility—the consistent demonstrtaion of skill and will.

Professors Steve Permuth and Robert Egley capture this admonition writing, "It takes careful and dedicated hard work and documentation to remove a teacher who is detrimental to the well-being of the school."[19] In spite of the barriers and challenges, the principal must put the needs of students first and bring courage to take the right position and use the right steps even in the face of the challenges.

School principals are central figures in the school tasked with the supervision and evaluation of teachers. With the use of proper documentation practices, principals and supervisors "can increase morale and minimize future legal problems."[20] Principals must possess and consistently apply the appropriate level of skills and knowledge of document imperative to only place and retain effective teachers in their classrooms.

NOTES

1. Vincent J. Connelly, Todd A. DeMitchell, & Douglas Gagnon, "Teacher Evaluation: Principal Perceptions of the Barriers to Dismissal Research, Policy, and Practice" *Education Law & Policy Review* 1 (2014): 172-92 175.

2. Susan Moore Johnson, *Teachers at Work: Achieving Success in Our Schools* (New York, NY: Basic Books 1990), xii.

3. Tim Hodges, "U.S. Superintendents Challenged to Find, Keep Good Teachers." *Gallup* (August 30, 2018), https://www.gallup.com/education/241796/superintendents-challenged-find-keep-good-teachers.aspx?g_source=link_NEWSV9&g_medium=TOPIC&g_campaign=item_&g_content=U.S.%2520Superintendents%2520Challenged%2520to%2520Find%2c%2520Keep%2520Good%2520Teachers.

4. Larry E. Frase, *Maximizing People Power in Schools: Motivating and Managing Teachers and Staff* (Newbury Park, CA: Corwin Press 1992), 72 (emphasis in original).

5. It is important to remember that the great majority, are as Ted Dintersmith, a venture capitalist and advocate for education, stated after his tour schools in all fifty, "are dedicated, passionate and committed—across all types of schools. They care." Ted Dintersmith, "Venture Capitalist Visits 200 Schools in 50 States and Says DeVos Is Wrong: If Choice and Competition Improve School, I found No Sign of It." *Answer Sheet, Washington Post* (March 15, 2019), https://www.washingtonpost.com/news/answer-sheet/wp/2018/03/15/heres-what-our-secretary-of-education-needs-to-hear-by-a-venture-capitalist-who-visited-200-schools-in-all-50-states/?utm_term=.e4179a319926.

6. *Robinson v. Morrill County. School District #63*, 910 N.W.2d 752, 767 (Neb. 2018).

7. Ibid.

8. Author DeMitchell suspended a teacher without pay for unprofessional conduct (inappropriate conduct with a student of flinging a student by his arm in removing a student from his seat in the auditorium). The teacher was more distressed about the written reprimand stating that he was involved in unprofessional conduct with a student than he was about the loss of pay.

9. Jeff Horner, "Fifteen Tips for Better Documentation of Employee Performance." *Education Law Reporter* 146 (2000): 613–616, 614.

10. "The cardinal rule of effective communication and documentation is to hold a conference first and write second." Kelly Frels, Janet L. Horton, Lisa McBride, and Ilya Feldsherov, *A Documentation System for Teacher Improvement or Termination* (7th Ed.) (Cleveland, OH: Education Law Association, 2014), 17.

11. Ibid. For example, to write, "Ms. Smith is a liar" is different than writing, "Ms. Smith was caught lying ten times."

12. See below for three examples citing to authority in documentation.
- "Furthermore, leaving a required meeting without prior permission is a violation of your job description as contained in Board Policy 4180 (D) and page 12 of the Faculty Handbook (copies are appended to this memorandum)."
- "Failure to heed this directive will result in further disciplinary action up to and including dismissal or non-renewal of your contract. Please see NRS 391.750 Grounds for suspension, demotion, dismissal, and refusal to reemploy teachers and administrators; consideration of evaluation and standards of performance as authority in this serious matter, a copy is appended."
- "This is the third time that you have arrived late at your classroom for your first period class in the last two weeks. I discussed your previous tardy attendance with you informally. You assured me that the problem would be addressed and that you would not leave your class unattended in the hallway. Article 4.4.2 of the collective bargaining agreement requires that you must be in your class for the start of school at least 15 minutes before the first period. You must follow the requirements of the collective bargaining agreement. Failure to follow this requirement may lead to a deficiency notice as well as a notice of insubordination. These notices may lead to further disciplinary action."

13. See *Freshwater v. Mt. Vernon City School District*, 1 N.E.3d 335, 343 (Ohio 2013) for an example of a directive regarding religious material in a public middle school science classroom that the Supreme Court of Ohio stated was "clear and unequivocal." The memorandum concludes, "Unless a particular discussion about religion or religious decorations or symbols is part of a Board approved curriculum, you may not engage in religious discussions with students while at school or keep religious materials displayed in the classroom." Ibid.

14. A New York Supreme Court, Appellate Division held that the documentation supporting a finding of unsatisfactory performance was neither "arbitrary nor capricious," thus upholding the dismissal. See *Meyers v. Department of Education of City of New York*, 55 N.Y.S.3d 17, 17 (A.D. 1 Dept. 2017) (writing, "The determination is

rationally supported by the principal's detailed descriptions of petitioner's difficulties in developing learning objectives, using lesson plans, maintaining academic rigor, meeting students' varying needs, facilitating 'accountable talk' through 'higher order thinking questions,' and actively engaging students, among other things as well as managing her classroom, and petitioner's persistent failure to improve despite the ongoing individualized professional development support she received.").

15. *Sanders v. Board of Education*, 263 N.W. 2d 461, 465 (Neb. 1978).

16. See *Brown v. Board of Education*, 347 U.S. 484, 491(1954) (writing, "Today, education is perhaps the most important function of state and local governments."); James Madison wrote, "Learned Institutions ought to be favorite objects with every free people. They throw that light over the public mind which is the best security against crafty & dangerous encroachments on the public liberty. They are the nurseries of skilful Teachers for the schools distributed throughout the Community. They are themselves schools for the particular talents required for some of the Public Trusts, on the able execution of which the welfare of the people depends.") James Madison, "Epilogue: Securing the Republic." Galliard Hunt (ed.), *The Writings of James Madison* 9(1900–1910): 103–109.

17. Marco A. Munoz and Florence C. Chang, "The Elusive Relationship Between Teacher Characteristics and Student Academic Growth: A Longitudinal Multilevel Model for Change." *Journal of Personnel Evaluation in Education* 20 (2007): 147–164, 147.

18. Jennifer K. Rice, *Teacher Quality: Understanding the Effectiveness of Teacher Attributes* (Washington, DC Economic Policy Institute 2003): v. Site visited February 28, 2019, available at http://www.epi.org/publications/entry/books_teacher_quality_execsum_intro/#ExecSum.

19. Steve Permuth and Robert Egley, "Letting Teachers Go—Legally." *Principal Leadership*, 3 (September 2002): 22–26, 26.

20. Horner, *supra* note 9, 616.

Appendix

TOOL BOX DOCUMENTS

The Tool Box Documents provide background information on evaluation and documentation. These documents can be used to inform and anchor policies and practices of school officials tasked with these important responsibilities.

DOCUMENT A

InTASC Model Core Teaching Standards and Learning Progressions for Teachers

The Council of Chief School Officers (CCSSO) defines a Model Core of Teaching Standards that all teachers must know and be able to do. It is an articulation of effective teaching that leads to improved student achievement. The Interstate Teacher Assessment and Support Consortium (InTASC) of the CCSO developed ten core standards for teachers without regard for subject or grade level. The ten core standards are organized into four general categories.

The Learner and Learning

Standard #1: Learner Development. The teacher understands how learners grow and develop, recognizing that patterns of learning and development vary individually within and across the cognitive, linguistic, social, emotional, and physical areas, and designs and implements developmentally appropriate and challenging learning experiences.

Standard #2: Learning Differences. The teacher uses understanding of individual differences and diverse cultures and communities to ensure inclusive learning environments that enable each learner to meet high standards.

Standard #3: Learning Environments. The teacher works with others to create environments that support individual and collaborative learning, and that encourage positive social interaction, active engagement in learning, and self-motivation.

Content

Standard #4: Content Knowledge. The teacher understands the central concepts, tools of inquiry, and structures of the discipline(s) he or she teaches and creates learning experiences that make the discipline accessible and meaningful for learners to assure mastery of the content.

Standard #5: Application of Content. The teacher understands how to connect concepts and use differing perspectives to engage learners in critical thinking, creativity, and collaborative problem solving related to authentic local and global issues.

Instructional Practice

Standard #6: Assessment. The teacher understands and uses multiple methods of assessment to engage learners in their own growth, to monitor learner progress, and to guide the teacher's and learner's decision making.

Standard #7: Planning for Instruction. The teacher plans instruction that supports every student in meeting rigorous learning goals by drawing upon knowledge of content areas, curriculum, cross-disciplinary skills, and pedagogy, as well as knowledge of learners and the community context.

Standard #8: Instructional Strategies. The teacher understands and uses a variety of instructional strategies to encourage learners to develop deep understanding of content areas and their connections, and to build skills to apply knowledge in meaningful ways.

Professional Responsibility

Standard #9: Professional Learning and Ethical Practice. The teacher engages in ongoing professional learning and uses evidence to continually evaluate his or her practice, particularly the effects of his or her choices and actions on others (learners, families, other professionals, and the community), and adapts practice to meet the needs of each learner.

Standard #10: Leadership and Collaboration. The teacher seeks appropriate leadership roles and opportunities to take responsibility for student learning, to collaborate with learners, families, colleagues, other school professionals, and community members to ensure learner growth, and to advance the profession.[1]

DOCUMENT B

Personnel Evaluation Standards

The Joint Committee on Standards for Educational Evaluation, created in 1975, developed in collaboration with major professional organizations in the United States and Canada standards that are widely reorganized. There are twenty-seven standards organized into four strands. All of the standards can be accessed through the website below. These standards provide a legal, fair, and accurate foundation for the development of an evaluation system as well as providing a guide for conducting evaluations. The four personnel evaluation strands are as follows:

> "*Propriety Standards* are intended to ensure that a personnel evaluation will be conducted legally, ethically, and with due regard for the welfare of the evaluate and those involved in the evaluation. [There are seven proprietary standards.]
>
> *Utility Standards* are intended to guide evaluations so that they will be informative, timely, and useful. [There are six utility standards.]
>
> *Feasibility Standards* are intended to guide personnel evaluation systems so that they are as easy to implement as possible, efficient in their use of time and resources, adequately funded, and viable from a political standpoint. [There are three feasibility standards.]
>
> *Accuracy Standards* determine whether an evaluation has produced sound information. Personnel evaluations must be technically adequate and as complete as possible to allow sound judgments and decisions to be made. The evaluation methodology should be appropriate for the purpose of the evaluation and the evaluatees being evaluated and the context in which they work. [There are eleven accuracy standards.]"[2]

DOCUMENT C

Examples of Causes and Evidence for Dismissal/Discipline

Court cases provide the application of causes for dismissal based on facts applied to rules such as state statutes, which define causes for dismissal. However, as mentioned above, professional standards are also articulated in other venues. For example, the prohibition against the verbal and physical abuse of students and faculty is found in other documents.[3] Furthermore, the National Education Association's Code of Ethics states, "In the fulfillment of the obligation to the student, the educator [s]hall not intentionally expose the student to embarrassment or disparagement."[4]

The following are examples from court cases regarding causes for dismissal. They may help to frame those actions that have given rise to dismissal and disciplinary proceedings against educators. The cases are divided into two major categories; those acts taking place during the employee's workday and associated with their daily responsibilities, and those that take place outside of the workday and have a questionable connection to professional responsibilities of the educator. In fact, it is this connection, this nexus between the questionable conduct and the impact on the education of the students, that frames the disposition of the case.

Selected In-School Activities Court Cases

- Ineffective planning and teaching.[5]
- "Inability to control her classroom, maintained questionable methods for determining students' grades, and required extraordinary assistance from school administrators and parents to enforce discipline"[6] supported a finding of incompetence, inefficiency, insubordination, and neglect of duty.
- Possession of a knife and gun placed in the teacher's desk by the teacher.[7]
- "The evidence showed that [teacher] was either unwilling or unable to implement suggestions and constructive criticism of her ineffectual teaching methods. She also continued to blame others and refused to accept any responsibility for her failure to provide a valid educational experience for her students and deliver consistently effective instruction."[8]
- Failure to follow reasonable administrative directions.[9]
- A coach was denied permission to purchase a new lawnmower for the sports field. He purchased it anyway with his own funds on behalf of the team. The principal authorized the purchase. The school board dismissed both when they learned of the purchase.[10]
- Failure to properly draft IEPs for students.[11]
- "The Constitution does not entitle teachers to present personal views to captive audiences against instructions of elected officials."[12]
- "A Pennsylvania court interpreted incompetency as deficiencies in personality, composure, judgment, and attitude that have a detrimental effect on a teacher's performance."[13]
- Promoting religious beliefs in the classroom.[14]
- A teacher kicked a kindergarten student with special needs and told the other students who witnessed the incident not to say anything.[15]
- The Ohio Department of Education refused to renew a teaching license based in part on inappropriate physical conduct with students by grabbing, jerking, and pushing them, and creating a hostile and negative learning and working environment.[16]
- A West Virginia teacher made sexual comments to many students and ignored warnings to cease this behavior.[17]
- Viewing adult pornographic material on-site using school district computer resources, even one time for just over one minute.[18]

- A well-respected high school science teacher of twenty-one years received an email from a fraternity brother during his planning period containing four pictures of a woman posing. In three of the pictures she was wearing a bikini but the fourth picture showed her bare breasts and pubic area.[19] Later that day he accessed the email in a colleague's classroom with students present. Although there was no showing that any students saw the email pictures, he eventually had his teaching certificate suspended for one year for conduct unbecoming to the profession.

Selected Out-of School Activities Court Cases

- Ineffectively serving as a role model for students.[20]
- Sexually related inappropriate conduct with students[21] or employees.[22]
- Multiple Driving Under the Influence (DUI) convictions constituted immorality/unfitness to teach.[23]
- Posting sexually explicit and pornographic photos of himself as part of his online advertisement for sexual partners.[24]
- An elementary school teacher who took pictures of five female students was convicted of five counts of sexual exploitation and three counts of sexual exploitation by a school employee. The pictures showed the female students in their underwear with exposed breasts. The teacher argued that the students were not currently his students and that he did not physically touch them and, thus, he could not violate that law. The Iowa court affirmed the district court finding that Romer was a school employee, the minors were students and that "no contemporaneous teacher-student was necessary," and photographing sexual contact between minors was sexual conduct.[25]
- A twenty-six-year-old female teacher was dismissed for texting a fourteen-year-old male student that she wanted him to be her boyfriend and invited him to her apartment where they kissed and petted. Sexually suggestive text messages followed, though there was no further physical contact.[26]
- A teacher placed pictures of his students near the pictures of naked men, and his email communications with his students were characterized as crossing the line of professional association with his students on the basis of his use of MySpace.[27]
- A school district's dismissal of a teacher based on a required drug test for cocaine was upheld. Reasonable suspicion was upheld based on the receipt correspondence between two attorneys regarding a custody dispute involving one of their teachers. The letter stated that the teacher had tested positive for cocaine use and that the teacher was not complying with a court order to undergo further drug testing. The school district investigated and required a drug test, which the teacher at first refused but later submitted to. The court found that there was reasonable suspicion at the inception of the search (the drug test) based on the following (1) the letter was based on

"personal, first-hand knowledge" of the drug test, (2) the drug test results were not obtained through hearsay but rather through a court order, and (3) combined with the letter's information was the teacher's "cavalier attitude at the outset" of the meeting. The dismissal was upheld based on a constitutionally firm search and seizure.[28]
- A North Carolina teacher was fired for possessing marijuana in his home even though the criminal charges were dropped.[29]
- A first grade teacher lost her appeal for her dismissal for posting on her Facebook page comments about her class. She posted the following, "I'm not a teacher—I'm a warden for future criminals!" and "They had a scared straight program in school—why couldn't [I] bring [first] graders?"[30]

DOCUMENT D

The Bologna Sandwich Technique

The Bologna Sandwich technique is indicative of an ineffective approach in which a supervisor seeks to say something positive about the teacher while essentially hiding or masking the most important part of the evaluation. The technique underscores the essential question , "where's the beef" in this evaluation.

DeMitchell first used this example when he worked with principals in his role of director of personnel and labor relations. Over the years, as the technique was tweaked, its source was unfortunately lost. The creative work of the originator of the Bologna Sandwich Technique in capturing how too often principals will slip into the position of wanting to say something positive, possibly as an anodyne for the teacher receiving the negative information, but to the detriment of the message of the evaluation is greatly appreciated. Unfortunately, we cannot give proper credit where credit is due.

Don't Do the Following

Burying the Message/The Bologna Sandwich
Technique in an Evaluation

Mr. A. has demonstrated a highly professional and tactful relationship with parents. He actively supports the parent association and volunteers many hours of extra work on its behalf.

His classroom is always neat. His bulletin boards are creative and tasteful. His room is visited by teachers from other schools because of his creativity.

He strikes students who disobey him. I have admonished him on many occasions that corporal punishment is contrary to district policy and the ethics of the profession. Records attached indicate that he has been observed hitting students on six different occasions during this academic year.

I received eight requests this year from parents to remove their child from Mr. A's classroom. This is more than all of the requests that I have received for the entire school.

Mr. A. spends many productive hours preparing for his classes. Lessons run smoothly and consistently capture the attention of his students. His questioning techniques are masterly, soliciting thoughtful, creative responses. His knowledge of the curriculum far exceeds the district's expectations.

I recommend Mr. A. for re-employment.

> Personnel decisions are clearly among the most complicated and complex ethical matters that educational administrators face. To whom is harm being done? Is it moral to keep an incompetent teacher and thus avoid harming him or her, while continuing to allow students to be harmed by his or her presence?[31]

DOCUMENT E

Negligent Hiring: Did We Hire the Wrong Person?[32]

The previous chapters and Tool Box Documents focused on the use of documentation during the course of employment. This Tool Box Document will take a look at the other end of the pipeline—the hiring process. Essentially, negligent hiring is a tort in which a person, in our discussion a student or an employee, was injured due to the negligence of the employer's hiring practice. Negligent hiring occurs at the entry point of employment. "An employer negligently hires an employee when it knew or should have known that the employee was unfit for the position."[33] The essential question is, Did the prospective employee pose a reasonably foreseeable risk of harm to others?[34]

If the employer failed to use due diligence in the hiring process, a lawsuit for negligent hiring may be successfully brought against the school district. Employing school districts that do not use care when hiring may face litigation if the employee later causes harm. Negligent hiring suits encourage employers to improve their investigative methods and techniques before placing employees in contact with students.[35]

In other words, school administrators should be able to document that they acted with due diligence in their hiring decision. "Such negligence usually consists of hiring or retaining the employee with knowledge of his unfitness, or failing to use reasonable care to discover it before hiring or retaining him."[36] Administrators responsible for hiring are in the best position to evaluate what is expected for the position and to judge the evidence/documents that form the basis for the hiring decision.

Schools should be held to high standards and be vigilant in the consistent application of prudent employment procedures because the selected teacher will be placed in situations of supervision over a vulnerable population, our children. The key element is whether the hiring process was diligent enough to reveal any reasonably foreseeable risk of harm that a prospective employee may present to students or other third parties.

Beck writes that in order to establish a *prima facie* claim for negligent hiring the following elements must be met:

(1) the defendant had a *duty* to exercise care in hiring;
(2) the defendant *breached* that duty by hiring an employee who was
    (a) *incompetent*, where
    (b) the defendant had *notice* of the employee's incompetence; and
(3) the defendant's hiring of the employee was a *proximate cause* of the plaintiff's injury.[37]

A prudent principal must review the employment application sections, the interview process, and the pre-employment investigation. Some suggestions are offered for each below. It should be kept in mind that a positive response to questions below should not be an automatic bar to employment unless the behavior is statutorily prohibited. The facts surrounding a positive response should be judged by the requirements of the position.

Sample Employment Application Sections

- "My signature below authorizes the school district to conduct a background investigation and authorizes release of information in connection with my application for employment."
- For the following questions add a place for the applicant's explanation. "If you answered "yes" to any of the following questions, provide date, incident, specific charge, city/state in which occurred:
  ◦ Have you ever been refused tenure or a continuing contract?
  ◦ Have you been discharged, suspended, or requested to resign from a teaching position?
  ◦ Have you ever had a certificate or license revoked or suspended?
  ◦ Are any criminal charges or proceedings pending against you?
  ◦ Has any court ever received a plea of guilty or a plea of *nolo contendere* from you for any offense involving moral turpitude (defined as an act of baseness, vileness or depravity in the private and social duties which a person owes another member of society in general and which is contrary to the accepted rule of right and duty between persons) deferred further proceedings without entering a finding of guilt or placed you on probation."

- "I certify that I have made true, correct, and complete answers and statements on this application in the knowledge that they may be relied upon in considering my application, and I understand that any material omission—falsely answered question made by me on this application or any supplement to it—will be sufficient grounds for failure to employ or for my discharge should I become employed with the school district."

Interview

- It is best to use an interviewing team so as to provide a variety of perspectives on the applicant's skills, knowledge, and demeanor.
- The interview team must be fully knowledgeable about the requirements for the position.
- Only those applicants that meet *all* of the requirements for the position should be invited to an interview.
- Review what questions are prohibited.[38]

Sample Pre-Employment Investigation for a Teacher

- Before a contract is offered, an administrator, or principal if applicable, from the personnel department must call the previous employer/principal or, if the candidate is a new teacher, the master teacher or university supervisor to do a reference check.
- A written record of who conducted the pre-employment investigation, who the investigator spoke to, and the date and time of the contact should be kept. The record can be kept in the personnel file if hired and confidentiality can be maintained since it a pre-employment inquiry, not available to the employee.
- Unless some specific questions arise during the interview, the investigator could ask the following questions from a prepared form and record the responses.
  - What is your name and position?
  - How long have you been acquainted with the applicant?
  - In what capacity did you know the applicant?
  - Did you directly supervise or observe the applicant performing his or her duties.
  - What are the strengths of the applicant?
  - How would you characterize the applicant's relationship with his or her students?
  - If we hire this applicant, in what area would you suggest that we provide additional inservicing or training?
  - Have there been any recent investigations concerning unprofessional conduct, incompetency, or immorality concerning this applicant?[39]
  - Would you rehire this individual if given the chance?

- Conduct any fingerprint and/or criminal background investigations that are available in your state.
- If any questions arise from the investigation, check further before offering a contract.

There are no magic formulas that can be written or incantations that can be invoked that will guarantee immunity from lawsuits. The decision to hire a specific teacher or employee may be one of the most important decisions made by principals and other administrators. The people in our schools make the school what it is and what it can become. Time, commitment, and knowledge must be invested in this crucial decision, not just to avoid liability but to secure the professional services of the best teachers available. Our students deserve no less effort on our part.

TABLE OF CASES

Preface

- *Cleveland Board of Education v. Loudermill*, 470 U.S. 532 (1985).
- *Plyler v. Doe*, 457 U.S. 202, 221 (1982).
- *Williams v. Stanton Common School District*, 173 Ky 798, 798 (1893).

Chapter 1: Evaluation and the Documentation Challenge

- *Adler v. Board. of Education.*, 342 U.S. 485 (1952).

Chapter 2: The Evaluation of Teachers

- *Briggs v. Board of Directors of Hinton Community School District*, 288 N.W.2d 740 (Iowa 1979).
- *Hayes v. Phoenix-Talent School District*, 893 F.2d 235 (9th Cir. 1990).
- *Iverson v. Wall Board. of Education.*, 522 N.W. 2d 188 (S.D. 1994).
- *Vernonia School District 47J v. Acton*, 515 U.S. 646 (1995).

Chapter 3: The Principal as Evaluator

- *Beggs v. Board of Education of Murphysboro Community Unit School District*, 72 N.E.3d 288 (2016).
- *Ekanem v. Greenville Public School*, 235 SO. 3d 1431, 1433 (Miss. App. 2017).
- *Kolmel v. City of New York*, 930 N.Y.S.2d 573, 574 (A.D. 1 Dept. 2011).

- *Spencer-East Brookfield Regional School District v. Spencer-East Brookfield Teachers' Assoc.*, 101 N.E.3d 305, 308 (Mass. App. Crt. 2018)

Chapter 4: The Legal Frameworks: Infusing Evaluation with Fairness

- *Armstrong v. Manzo*, 380 U.S. 545, 552 (1965).
- *Board of Regents v. Roth*, 408, U.S. 564 (1972).
- *Cafeteria Workers v. McElroy*, 367 U.S. 886, 895 (1961).
- *Cleveland Board of Education. v. Loudermill*, 470 U.S. 532, 546–48 (1985).
- *County of Sacramento v. Lewis*, 523 U.S. 833, 845 (1998).
- *Doe v. Baum*, 903 F.3d 575 (6th Cir. 2018).
- *Donahoo v. Board of Education*, 109 N.E. 2d 787, 789 (Ill. 1952).
- Enterprise Wire Company and Enterprise Independent Union, 46 LA 359 (1964).
- *Ferraro v. Farina*, 69 N.Y.S. 3d 266, 267 (A.D. 1 Dept. 2017).
- *Fritz v. Evers*, 907 F.3d 533, 534 (7th Cir. 2018).
- *Gideon v. Wainwright*, 372 U.S. 335 (1963).
- *Goldberg v. Kelly*, 397 U.S. 254 (1970).
- *Griggsville-Perry School District*, 127 LA 1542 (2010).
- *Hamerski v. Belleville Area Special Services Cooperative*, 302 F.Supp. 3d 992, 1001 (S.D. Ill. 2018).
- *Hampton v. United States*, 425 U.S. 484 (1976).
- *Hortonville Joint School District No. 1 v. Hortonville Education Association*, 426 U.S. 482 (1976).
- *Houston Federation of Teachers, Local 2415 v. Houston Independent. School District*, 251 F. Supp. 3d 1168, 1176 (S.D. Tex. 2017). 262 (1978).
- *Morrissey v. Brewer*, 408 U.S. 471, 481 (1972).
- *Mullane v. Central Hanover Bank & Trust Co.*, 339 U.S. 306, 314 (1950).
- *Nobile v. Board of Education of the City School District of the City of New York*, 89 N.Y.S. 3d 137 (A.D. 1 Dept. 2018).
- *Paul v. Davis*, 424 U.S. 693, 711 (1976).
- *Pollard v. Board of Education Reorganized School District No. III*, 533 S.W. 2d 667, 670 (Mo. Ct. App. 1976).
- *Rochin v. California*, 342 U.S. 165 (1972).

Chapter 5: The Fatal "Eyes" of Unprofessional Conduct

- *Ambach v. Norwick*, 441 U.S. 68 (1979).
- *Board of Education of West Yuma School District RJ-1 v. Flaming*, 938 P.2d 151 (Colo. 1997).
- *Cona v. Avondale School District*, 842 N.W. 2d 277 (2013).

- *Crosby v. Holt*, 320 S.W. 3d 805 (Tenn. Ct. App. 2009).
- *DeYoung v. Commission on Professional Competence*, 228 Cal. App. 4th 568 (2014).
- *Horosko v. School District of Mount Pleasant Township*, 6 A. 2d 866, (1939).
- *Lackow v. Department of Education of the City of New York*, 51 A.D. 3d 563 (N.Y.A.D. 1 Dept. 2008).
- *McBroom v. Board of Education, District No. 205*, 494, N.E. 2d 1191 (App. Crt. 2 Dist. 1986).
- *McKay v. State ex rel. Young*, 212 Ind. 338 (1937).
- *Morrison v. State Board of Education* 461 P.2d 375 (Cal. 1969).
- (*Munroe v. Central Bucks School District*, 34 F. Supp. 3d 532 (E.D. Pa. 2014))
- *Rolando v. School Directors of District No. 125*, 358 N.E.2d 945 (3rd Dist. 1976).
- *San Diego Unified School District v. Commission on Professional Competence*, 124 Cal. Rptr. 3d 320 (App. 4 Dist. 2011).
- *Thomas v. Board of Education of Cape Girardeau School District No. 63*, 926 S.W. 2d 163 (Mo. Ct. App. 1996).

Chapter 6: Files, Memos, and Documentation
- *Bain v. Wrend*, 2018 WL 5980376 (November 14, 2018).
- *Cohen v. Board of Education of City School District*, 960 N.Y.S.2d 362 (A.D. 1 Dept. 2013).
- *Moss v. Texarkana Arkansas School District*, 240 F.Supp.3d, 966 (W.D. Ark. 2017).
- *NLRB v. J. Weingarten Co.*, 420 U.S. 251 (1975).
- *Orth v. Phoenix High School System*, 613 P.2d 311 (Ariz. Ct. App. 1980).
- *Timpani v. Lakeside School Dist.*, 386 S.W.3d 588 (Ark. App. 2011).
- *Vergra v. State*, No. BC484642, 2014 WL 2598719 (Cal. Super. Ct. L.A. Cty. June 10, 2014).

Chapter 7: Conclusion and the Ten Commandments of Documentation
- *Brown v. Board of Education*, 347 U.S. 484 (1954).
- *Freshwater v. Mt. Vernon City School District*, 1 N.E.3d 335, 343 (Ohio 2013).
- *Meyers v. Department of Education of City of New York*, 55 N.Y.S.3d 17, 17 (A.D. 1 Dept. 2017).
- *Robinson v. Morrill County. School District #63*, 910 N.W.2d 752 (Neb. 2018).
- *Sanders v. Board of Education*, 263 N.W. 2d 461 (Neb. 1978).

Toolbox Document C Examples of Causes and Evidence for Dismissal/Discipline

- *Ambach v. Norwick*, 441 U.S. 68 (1979).
- *Benjamin v. N.Y. City Bd./Dept. of Educ.*, 964 N.Y.S.2d 139 (A.D. 1 2013).
- *Broney v. California Commission on Teacher Credentialing*, 108 Cal. Rptr.3d 832 (Cal.App. 3 Dist. 2010).
- *Brown v. City of New York,* 2017 NY Slip Op 50068(U) (Sup. Crt. NY Cnty Jan. 19, 2017).
- *Bui v. Chippewa Local School District Board of Educ*ation, 9th Dist. Wayne No. 2924, 1995 WL 542217 (Sept. 13, 1995).
- *Childs v. Roane County Board of Education*, 929 S.W. 2d 364 (Tenn. App. 1996).
- *Doe v. St. Francis School District,* 694 F.3d 869 (7th Cir. 2012).
- *Hamburg v. North Pennsylvania School District*, 484 A.2d 867 (Pa. Commw. Ct. 1984)
- *Gongora v. New York City Department of Education,* 951 N.Y.S.2d 137 (A.D. 1 Dept. 2012).
- *Haas v New York City Department of Education*, 966 N.Y.S. 2d 397 (N.Y. App. Div. 2013).
- *Harry v. Marion County School Board*, 203 W. Va. 64 (1998).
- *Hester v. Lowndes County School District*, 137 So. 3d 325 (Miss. Ct. App. 2013).
- *In the Matter of the Tenure Hearing of Jennifer O'Brien,* Superior Court of New Jersey, Appellate Division, No. A-2452-11T4 (January 11, 2013) (slip. op.).
- *In re Freeman*, 426 S.E. 2d 100 (N.C. Ct. App. 1993).
- *Khachatourian v. Hacienda La Puente Unified School Dis*trict, 572 Fed. Appx. 556 (9th Cir. 2014).
- *Langdon v. Ohio Department of Education*, 87 N.E. 3d (Ohio App. 12 Dist. 2017).
- *Mayer v. Monroe County Community School Corporation*, 474 F.3d 477, 479–80 (7th Cir. 2007).
- *Metz v. Bethlehem Area School District*, 177 A.3d 384 (Pa. Commy. Ct. 2018).
- *Moffitt v. Tunkhannock Area School District*, 192 A.3d 1214 (Pa. Comwlth. 2018).
- *Rhoades v. Laurel Highlands School District*, 544 A.2d 562 (Pa. Comwlth. 1988).
- *Robinson v. Ohio Department of Education*, 971 N.E.2d 977 (Ohio App. 2 Dist. 2012).
- *San Diego Unified School District v. Commission on Professional Competence*, 124 Cal.Rptr.3d 320 (Cal.App. 4 Dist. 2011).
- *Spanierman v. Hughes*, 576 F. Supp. 2d 292 (D. Conn. 2008).

- *State v. Romer*, 832 N.W. 2d 169, 184 (Iowa, 2013).
- *Tingley v. Vaughn*, 17 Ill. App. 347 (1885).
- *Villada v. City of New York*, 6 N.Y.S.3d 52, 53 (A.D. 1 Dept. 2015).
- *Webb v. South Panola School District*, 101 S. 3d 724 (Miss. Ct. App. 2012).
- *Zellner v. Herrick*, 639 F.3d 371 (7th Cir. 2011).

Tool Box Document E Negligent Hiring: Did We Hire the Wrong Person?

- *Anderson v. Soap Lake School District*, 423 P. 3d 197, 206 (Wash. 2018).

NOTES

1. Interstate Teacher Assessment and Support Consortium, InTASC *Model Core Teaching Standards and Learning Progressions for Teachers 1.0: A Resource for Ongoing Teacher Development.* (Washington, DC: Council of Chief State School Officers, April 2013), 8–9.

2. Author, *Personnel Evaluation Standard.* Joint Committee on Standards for Educational Evaluations, (Kalamazoo, MI: The Evaluation Center). Site visited June 8, 2019 available at http://www.jcsee.org/personnel-evaluation-standards.

3. Representative Assembly, *Code of Ethics* (Washington, DC: National Education Association 1975) Site visited February 24, 2019, available at http://www.nea.org/home/30442.htm.

4. Ibid.

5. See *Brown v. City of New York,* 2017 NY Slip Op 50068(U) (Sup. Crt. NY Cnty Jan. 19, 2017) (finding ineffective teaching by documentation on lack of understanding of a range of pedagogical approaches, managing classroom procedures and routines, loss of instructional time, and confusing and unclear instruction.

6. *Childs v. Roane County Board of Education*, 929 S.W. 2d 364, 365-66 (Tenn. App. 1996).

7. *Khachatourian v. Hacienda La Puente Unified School District*, 572 Fed. Appx. 556 (9th Cir. 2014).

8. *Benjamin v. N.Y. City Bd./Dept. of Educ.*, 964 N.Y.S.2d 139, 140 (A.D. 1 2013).

9. *Bui v. Chippewa Local Sch. Dist. Bd. of Educ.*, 9th Dist. Wayne No. 2924, 1995 WL 542217 (Sept. 13, 1995) in which the teacher resisted making any changes suggested by the school principal over a two-year period to alleviate excess noise and disorder in his classroom.

10. *Hester v. Lowndes County School District*, 137 So. 3d 325 (Miss. Ct. App. 2013).

11. *Webb v. South Panola School District*, 101 S. 3d 724 (Miss. Ct. App. 2012).

12. *Mayer v. Monroe County Community School Corporation*, 474 F.3d 477, 479-80 (7th Cir. 2007).

13. Martha M. McCarthy, Nelda Cambron-McCabe, and Suzanne E. Eckes, Public School Law: Teacher 367 (2014) (Boston: Pearson) (citing *Hamburg v. North Pennsylvania School District*, 484 A.2d 867 (Pa. Commw. Ct. 1984) (writing, "Incompetency in this case was supported by evidence that the teacher was a disruptive influence on the school; could not maintain control of students, and failed to maintain her composure in dealing with students, other professionals, and parents."). Ibid.

14. *Rhoades v. Laurel Highlands School District*, 544 A.2d 562 (Pa.Cmwlth. 1988).

15. *Haas v New York City Department of Education*, 966 N.Y.S. 2d 397 (N.Y. App. Div. 2013).

16. *Langdon v. Ohio Department of Education*, 87 N.E. 3d (Ohio App. 12 Dist. 2017).

17. *Harry v. Marion County School Board*, 203 W. Va. 64 (1998).

18. *Zellner v. Herrick*, 639 F.3d 371 (7th Cir. 2011).

19. *Robinson v. Ohio Department of Education*, 971 N.E.2d 977, 980 (Ohio App. 2 Dist. 2012). The Licensure Code of Professional Conduct for Ohio Educators stated in pertinent part, "(g) Using technology to intentionally host or post improper or inappropriate material that could be reasonably be accessed by the school community." Ibid., 982.

20. See *Ambach v. Norwick*, 441 U.S. 68, 78-9 (1979) ("a teacher serves as a role model for [his/her] students, exerting a subtle but important influence over their values and perceptions"; *Tingley v. Vaughn*, 17 Ill. App. 347, 351 (1885) ("If suspicion of vice or immorality be once entertained against a teacher, his influence for good is gone. The parents become distrustful, the pupils contemptuous and school discipline essential to success is at an end"); *In Re Appeal of Morrill*, 145 N.H. 692, 704) (2001) (holding that credential revocation was properly revoked for lack of good moral character.)

21. See *Gongora v. New York City Department of Education*, 951 N.Y.S.2d 137, 139 (A.D. 1 Dept. 2012) (dismissing teacher for sexual misconduct for phoning an eighteen-year-old student at home to ask her to go on a date before she graduated).

22. See *Villada v. City of New York*, 6 N.Y.S.3d 52, 53 (A.D. 1 Dept. 2015) (supporting the termination of an employee for his sexual misconduct toward another teacher through his unwanted touching and kissing).

23. *Moffitt v. Tunkhannock Area School District,* 192 A.3d 1214 (Pa. Comwlth. 2018) (dismissing a principal on the basis of immorality); *Broney v. California Commission on Teacher Credentialing*, 108 Cal. Rptr.3d 832 (Cal.App. 3 Dist. 2010) (upholding unfitness to teach as just cause for suspending teacher's teaching credential).

24. *San Diego Unified School District v. Commission on Professional Competence*, 124 Cal.Rptr.3d 320 (Cal.App. 4 Dist. 2011).

25. *State v. Romer*, 832 N.W. 2d 169, 184 (Iowa, 2013). The legislative intent, the court asserted, was that the term school employee encompassed employees, such as principals, or custodians, who do not have a student-teacher relationship and that its intent was to criminalize power relationships. Ibid.,177–78.

26. *Doe v. St. Francis School District*, 694 F.3d 869, 871 (7th Cir. 2012). The teacher was fired, prosecuted, and plead guilty to fourth-degree sexual assault. Ibid.

The student sued the school district under Title IX but lost, failing to demonstrate that the school district had actual notice of the misconduct and failed to reasonably investigate the allegation. Ibid., 871–72.

27. *Spanierman v. Hughes*, 576 F. Supp. 2d 292 (D. Conn. 2008).

28. *Metz v. Bethlehem Area School District*, 177 A.3d 384, 393 (Pa. Commw. Ct. 2018).

29. *In re Freeman*, 426 S.E. 2d 100 (N.C. Ct. App. 1993).

30. *In the Matter of the Tenure Hearing of Jennifer O'Brien*, Superior Court of New Jersey, Appellate Division, No. A-2452-11T4 (January 11, 2013) (slip. op.) at *2.

31. David W. Messer, *The Impact of Dismissal of Non-Tenured Teachers on Principals in Tennessee* (East Tennessee State University: Unpublished doctoral dissertation 2001), 17. Site visited June 16, 2019, available at https://dc.etsu.edu/cgi/viewcontent.cgi?article=1135&context=etd.

32. This Tool Box Document is adapted from Todd A. DeMitchell, "Negligent Hiring: Did We Hire the Wrong Person? (Chapter 7) *Negligence: What Principals Need to Know about Avoiding Liability* (Lanham, MD: Rowman & Littlefield Education, 2007): 61–66. Used with the permission of the author.

33. *Anderson v. Soap Lake School District*, 423 P. 3d 197, 206 (Wash. 2018).

34. Kelly M. Feeley, "Hiring Sexters to Teach Children: Creating Predictable and Flexible Standards for Negligent Hiring in Schools" *New Mexico Law Review* 42 (2012): 83–130, 93.

35. Ibid., 129.

36. 53 Am. Jur. 2d Master and Servant § 422 (1970).

37. Jeremy Beck, "Entity Liability for Teacher-on-Student Sexual Harassment: Could State Law Offer Greater Protection Than Federal Statutes?" *Journal of Law & Education* 35 (2006): 141–147, 145 (2006) (emphasis in original).

38. See U.S. Equal Employment Opportunity Commission available at https://www.eeoc.gov/laws/practices/index.cfm.

39. Behaviors such as unprofessional conduct, incompetency, or immorality may make the applicant unsuitable for employment as a teacher. See Shawn D. Vance, "How Reforming the Tort of Negligent Can Enhance the Economic Activity of a State, Be Good for Business and Protect the Victim" *Legislation and Policy Brief*, 6 (2014): 171–213, 202 writing, "information regarding whether the applicant had engaged in behavior that would meet the definition of unsuitable for employment listed in this provision, to specifically include violent actions towards co-workers, customers of the employer, and/or any other person to whom the applicant came into contact by virtue of his or her employment with the previous employer."

About the Authors

Todd A. DeMitchell (BA/MAT, University of La Verne; MA, University of California, Davis; EdD, University of Southern California; and Post-Doctorate, Harvard Graduate School of Education) is the John & H. Irene Peters professor of education and professor of justice studies, where he previously held the Lamberton professorship of justice studies, at the University of New Hampshire. He was also selected as Distinguished Professor of the University and he received an excellence in teaching award as well as being named as a Kimball faculty fellow. Prior to joining the faculty at the University of New Hampshire, he spent eighteen years in the public schools as an elementary school teacher, principal (K–8), director of personnel and labor relations (K–12), and superintendent (K–8). In these various positions, he had direct responsibility for the evaluation of the faculty. He has published eight books. He has over 200 publications including law reviews, peer-reviewed journals, professional journals, chapters, and commentaries. His research has been cited in top law school law reviews, in peer-reviewed journals, and in cases and motions before state and federal courts including the U.S. Supreme Court.

Mark A. Paige (BA, Tufts University-*magna cum laude*; MS, J.D.-*cum laude*. PhD, University of Wisconsin-Madison) is an associate professor of public policy at the University of Massachusetts-Dartmouth. Before joining the faculty at the University of Massachusetts, he was a practicing school law attorney representing school districts in New England in all aspects of school law, including special education, labor relations, and employment law. He appeared before state and federal jurisdictions, including the New Hampshire

Supreme Court. He has published numerous law reviews and peer-reviewed journal articles on education law. In addition, Rowman & Littlefield published his book *Building a Better Teacher: Understanding Value-Added in the Law of Teacher Evaluation* (2016). He began his career as a fifth-grade teacher in Austin, Texas.

www.ingramcontent.com/pod-product-compliance
Lightning Source LLC
Chambersburg PA
CBHW021215240426

43672CB00026B/318